Morrill Wyman

Autumnal catarrh

Hay fever

Morrill Wyman

Autumnal catarrh
Hay fever

ISBN/EAN: 9783337372347

Printed in Europe, USA, Canada, Australia, Japan

Cover: Foto ©Thomas Meinert / pixelio.de

More available books at **www.hansebooks.com**

AUTUMNAL CATARRH

(*HAY FEVER*)

WITH THREE MAPS

BY

MORRILL WYMAN, M. D.

LATE HERSEY PROFESSOR ADJUNCT OF THE THEORY AND PRACTICE OF MEDICINE
IN HARVARD UNIVERSITY.

NEW YORK
PUBLISHED BY HURD AND HOUGHTON
The Riverside Press, Cambridge
1872

To

JEFFRIES WYMAN, M. D.,

PROFESSOR OF ANATOMY IN HARVARD UNIVERSITY,

THIS ESSAY

IS AFFECTIONATELY INSCRIBED.

ONE of the most interesting questions connected with Autumnal Catarrh is its geographical distribution. Much valuable information has already been received, for which I would express my thanks. More facts bearing upon this point are much desired. To Professor Arnold Guyot, of Princeton, I am indebted for the use of his excellent physical maps of New England and the Eastern United States, upon which to lay down the catarrhal regions as at present known ; also to the publishers of Starr King's " White Hills," for similar facilities as to the White Mountain regions.

CAMBRIDGE, *June*, 1872.

CONTENTS.

ERRATA.

Page 2. For "Heywood," read " Hayward."
Page 72. For " 2,212," read " 3,212."

AUTUMNAL CATARRH.

INTRODUCTION.

§ 1. In the northern part of the United States of America there are two distinct forms of annually returning catarrh. One known as the " Rose Cold," or " June Cold," commencing during the last week in May or the first week in June, and continuing until about the first week in July. This corresponds in most of its symptoms and in the time of attack with that popularly known in England as " Hay Fever," or " Hay Asthma."

Hay Fever, as it exists in England, was first described by Dr. John Bostock, in 1819, in the tenth and fourteenth volumes of the " Medico-Chirurgical Transactions," under the name of *Catarrhus Æstivus*.[1] He had collected twenty-eight cases, ten of them " less correctly ascertained," from which, and from his own personal sufferings, he drew his description of the disease. Since then, numerous treatises, more or less complete, have been published in England, France, Germany, and Switzerland.

Dr. Phœbus of Giessen [2] has collected the cases described in these treatises, and, by means of circulars addressed to various physicians, obtained much other information.

[1] John Bostock, " Catarrhus Æstivus," or " Summer Catarrh ; " *Medico-Chirurgical Transactions*, vol. x. p. 161, and vol. xiv. p. 437.

[2] *Der typische Frühsommer-Katarrh oder das sogenannte Heufieber, Heu-Asthma*, von Philip Phœbus, Giessen, 1862.
The Typical Early Summer Catarrh, or the so-called Hay Fever, Hay Asthma, by Philip Phœbus, Giessen, 1862.

From these materials, without apparently having treated or personally investigated the disease in his own practice, he has drawn up the most systematic work upon the subject which has yet appeared.

Although this disease in the time of its access, its duration, and in most of its symptoms, resembles that which exists in the United States, I am not aware of any certain evidence of the identity of the two diseases, at least so far as the causes are concerned. Nor do I know of any persons who, having suffered from an annual catarrh here in June, have suffered in other years from a similar disease at the same season in England. On the other hand, I have known those who having suffered here in June, have subsequently been in England or on the Continent during the same month and entirely escaped any similar disease. Two cases of the June Catarrh as occurring here will be described further on as a means of comparison.

The other form, which occurs in autumn, has attracted very little attention; and, I believe, has been pretty generally, both by sufferers and physicians, confounded with ordinary occasional catarrh, or with the " Hay Cold " or " June Cold " just mentioned.

In examining the work of Dr. Phœbus, I find one case, contributed by the late Dr. George Heywood of Boston, which is considered by Dr. Phœbus as differing from the others in his collection, and is therefore rejected from his list. Further inquiries have satisfied me that this case belongs to the second form.

§ 2. I had long been a sufferer from this last disease, but have never yet met with a description of it in any medical work. In 1854 it was described by me in my course of lectures in the Medical School of Harvard University; the description being drawn from my personal experience, and the few cases which had come under my observation for treatment. This, so far as I know, is the first published description of the affection.

In May, 1866, the facts then known to me were embodied in a paper read at the annual meeting of the Massachusetts Medical Society in Boston.[1] Subsequently I made more exact inquiries of physicians and others. Of the physicians to whom I applied, very few had met with or ever heard of the disease, and doubted its existence except as an ordinary catarrh. Three physicians, however, had cases occurring either in their own persons or families, from whom careful histories were obtained. But by far the greater part of the knowledge I now have is from a personal examination of the subjects of the disease, the de-

[1] The following abstract was published in the *Boston Journal*, June 2, 1866 : —

AUTUMNAL CATARRH. — At the meeting of the Massachusetts Medical Society, Dr. Wyman of Cambridge gave an account of a singular catarrhal affection, or cold, hitherto undescribed, and named by him Autumnal Catarrh. There are two annually recurring catarrhs in this country : the summer catarrh (commonly called Rose Cold, Hay Fever, or June Cold) begins the last week in May or the first week in June, and lasts four or five weeks ; the other, the Autumnal Catarrh, commences the last week in August, and continues till the last week in September. It begins with sneezing, itching of the eyes, especially at the inner corners, watering of the eyes, and a profuse discharge from the nostrils. The affection of the eyes is in fits, coming on suddenly, compelling the sufferer to rub his eyes violently for relief. The fits of sneezing and nose-blowing and obstruction of the nostrils are also sudden, and when the fit is over, usually in a few minutes, go off as quick as they came. During the second week in September, a cough sets in, dry, violent, and in fits ; it is increased by dry, dusty weather, and relieved by an easterly storm. It is most severe in the night, and there is sometimes asthma. The disease subsides during the third week in September, and by the first of October, or the first good frost, is entirely gone. It is not an uncommon disease ; Daniel Webster had it annually for twenty years, and while Secretary of State suggested to President Fillmore the propriety of resigning on account of it. The late Chief Justice of Massachusetts was another victim. Medicines seem to have been most freely tried without materially relieving its severity or shortening its duration. Fortunately, it has been ascertained that there is a most complete and agreeable cure. Within twenty-four hours after the sufferer arrives at the White Mountains, at Gorham, at the Glen House, or the Waumbec, it suddenly disappears, and does not return for that year, if he remains till the last week in September, the usual time of disappearance. The relief at Franconia is not so certain as at the north side of the mountains, though most are relieved there also.

scription being written down and carefully corrected in
their presence.   A few cases have been communicated by
letter, generally containing a full account of the symptoms, with the effects of place, season, and other physical
influences.

Several illustrative cases are given in full, and eighty-
three are collected in a Tabular View at the end of the
volume. This contains the principal symptoms in groups.
First, those of the head, nose, eyes, ears, and throat.
Second, those of the chest, cough, difficulty of breathing,
and condition of heart ; the severity, in each case, being
indicated. To these are added the time of beginning and
end of the annual attack and the influence of locality.
Other cases have come to my knowledge, but the histories
are not sufficiently full for my purpose.

The number of cases collected and the completeness of
the histories, derived as they are from various parts of the
northern section of the United States, and comprising the
most common forms of the affection, will warrant me in
giving a general description which shows, I think, that the
disease differs from any heretofore described.

§ 3. To this disease I propose to give the name of *Catarrhus Autumnalis* or *Autumnal Catarrh*, in conformity
with the nomenclature of Dr. Bostock, and because it in-
volves no theory as to its cause, of which very little is
known.

The popular name, " Hay Fever," is objectionable.   It
was first used by Dr. Bostock about 1824, to designate the
English disease.   In this country it has been applied to
the " June Cold " or " Rose Cold."   As indicating this
disease it is certainly inappropriate, if it is intended
thereby to indicate that it is caused in any way by hay.
The hay in New England has generally been cut and got
in a month before its appearance, and it is only in exceptional cases that the smell or dust of hay, any more than

any other dust, produces uncomfortable sensations in the subjects of this disease.

" Hay Asthma," another popular name, indicates that difficult breathing is the main symptom. But this it certainly is not. The affections of the eyes and nose are more frequent and more constant. If it is intended to indicate the cause, it is as objectionable as " Hay Fever."

Bronchitis has been proposed, but this implies, first, that it is an inflammation, and secondly, that its principal seat is in the air tubes. That it is an ordinary inflammation can hardly be maintained, neither is its principal seat in the air tubes. This term, therefore, is objectionable.

The term Catarrh, on the other hand, indicates a condition of the mucous membrane, accompanied by a flow of a thin secretion, not necessarily implying inflammation ; this is what we find in the disease before us ; it is, indeed, the most prominent symptom.

Objection may be made to the word Autumnal, inasmuch as the astronomical autumn does not commence till about the 22d of September, at which time the disease has nearly finished its course. But popularly in the United States, the three autumnal months are September, October, and November ; in England, August is reckoned as the first month of autumn.

The name, Autumnal Catarrh, here adopted, seems, therefore, to be as little objectionable as any which has been proposed. It indicates two important facts connected with the disease, and presents no theory.

My investigations have necessarily been made, in a great measure, in New England. Care has been taken, however, to push my inquiries as far as possible into the Southern and Western States, through sufferers who have been there during the critical period. The disease requires further investigation, and it is to be hoped that it will be made in these directions. I now proceed to the general history.

§ 4. My principal object in this paper is to give as accurately as may be the *Natural History* of this singular disease ; its origin, course, and termination ; its relation to seasons and places ; and the influence of various physical agents either in producing it as a whole or in exciting paroxysms of suffering.

An outline or general history will be given in this section ; the symptoms, with cases, will be found further on.

All the cases agree in the time of annual return, about the 20th of August, varying but a few days from this date in different years. In some individuals it is remarkably punctual, being first noticed on precisely the same day of the month, and it is even asserted, at the same hour of the day.

It is first perceived as a slight itching in the palate and in the parts about the roof of the mouth, soon followed by similar sensations, apparently in the eustachian tube, extending from the throat into the ears, and inducing the sufferer to attempt relief by swallowing, and rubbing his tongue against the back part of the hard palate, and by pressing and rubbing the external orifice of the ear to give motion to the parts within.

There is often a sense of tension about the forehead, especially over the eyes in the region of the frontal sinuses.

In a day or two the nostrils are affected ; there is irritation of the lining membrane, sneezing, and a stuffing and obstruction of the nostrils. This obstruction is peculiar ; it occurs in paroxysms of short duration, one or both nostrils becoming suddenly obstructed, and in two or three minutes as suddenly relieved; at other times the obstruction is more prolonged. But, however complete, it is, in many individuals, almost immediately relieved by active exercise, rapid walking, leaping, or any movement, indeed, which gives warmth to the extremities.

At first these attacks occur only in the morning or on first rising; as the disease advances they occur later in the day, but still in short paroxysms.

At this stage the discharge from the nostrils is limpid and almost free from mucus; it is often very copious, especially during or immediately following attacks of sneezing. Holding down the head is often accompanied by a rapid dropping of the same fluid without sneezing.

With this trouble in the nostrils comes watering of the eyes and itching along the edge of the lids and in the conjunctiva generally, but most at the inner corner. This irritation is also in paroxysms of a few minutes' duration, and so intense that it is almost impossible for the sufferer to refrain from rubbing the eye balls violently,—which soon relieves them, notwithstanding that such treatment increases the turgidity of the vessels until the whole conjunctival surface becomes of a nearly uniform red. The eyelids are swollen, their edges red and inflamed; the the small glands are also inflamed, and in some cases pustules or sties form and break, leaving an excoriated surface which heals slowly. The whole face is often red and swollen, especially in the morning.

The senses of taste and smell are much impaired, and in some cases almost abolished, and at times there is partial deafness with a sense of obstruction of the internal ear. The lining membrane of the external tube is sometimes much irritated, even to the extent of producing a thin discharge, without evidence of the irritation extending to the tissue beneath.

Deglutition is interfered with, especially when the nostrils are so obstructed as to prevent the perfect motion of the parts necessary to this act. The mucous membrane of the mouth, tonsils, and pharynx partakes of the general irritation, and becomes red ; and sometimes there is soreness of the throat. The lips become dry, cracked, and swollen.

The skin is easily irritated and excoriated, and the excoriations are not as readily healed as in health. Many also suffer from itching of the skin, especially on the scalp, back, and chest, at times accompanied by a slight papular eruption.

During some portion of this period there is chilliness, or rather sensitiveness to cold ; more or less pain, or sense of oppression in the head ; the appetite diminishes ; there is lassitude and weakness. The pulse is accelerated and weakened, the skin hot and dry, with other signs of a febrile movement.

Towards the end of the second week, to these symptoms is added irritation of the bronchial mucous membrane ; a frequent and dry cough, commencing with a sense of tickling in the upper part of the windpipe, but little relieved by the cough, or only after long coughing, and the expectoration of a small quantity of transparent glairy mucus. The severity of the bronchial symptoms depends much upon the condition of the atmosphere ; if dry and dusty, the cough is much worse ; dampness and a rain-storm give relief. During the third week the affection of the lungs gradually increases ; the cough, still with very little expectoration, is more troublesome, especially in the night, sometimes compelling the patient to spend an hour or two sitting up, and not unfrequently is spasmodic in its character, producing convulsive retching or even vomiting.

The disease may now be assumed to be at its height. It is in this stage also that in some cases asthmatic symptoms appear ; and although they are sometimes severe, are not usually long continued.

At the end of the third week the catarrhal symptoms

diminish, the tickling of the fauces ceases, the eyes and nose improve; but the cough is apt to continue longer, and the heart's action is easily accelerated by exercise, and the pulse sometimes intermitting. The skin is dry, and warmer than natural.

During the fourth week in September these symptoms gradually diminish, and by the end of September, or the first frost, are nearly gone, leaving weakness, and a more or less altered state of the mucous membrane, the effect of the prolonged irritation, from which the patient (if otherwise in good health) generally soon recovers.

§ 5. Such is the usual course of the disease. All the symptoms are seldom present in the same individual. The symptoms connected with the head; the itching of the eyes, ears, nose, and fauces varies in severity, but is never wanting. The cough is also variable, but occurs in most. The asthma is the least frequent, although, when present, it is sometimes severe. In some there is a daily paroxysm of fever, accompanied by headache, intolerance of light, and debility, compelling the patient to keep his room, or even his bed, for several days in succession. It varies somewhat in severity in different years; enough to encourage sanguine individuals in the belief that their last new remedy is at length effectual. The tendency of this annually repeated affection of the mucous membrane is to prolong the disease into cold weather, and, in some rare instances, to bring about a permanent chronic bronchitis, gradually undermining the health. In some individuals, again, the action of the heart is more or less interfered with, which may have had an influence in some of the cases recorded, in shortening life, or determining the kind of death.

THE NOSE.

§ 6. THE lining membrane of the nostrils is the part first affected ; beginning with a slight tickling or itching, which soon shoots upward towards the eyes, and even into them. These sensations gradually increase as the parts become more irritated, and are accompanied by a slight moisture of the nostrils.

In a short time sneezing commences of a most extraordinary kind.[1] The sneeze is seldom single ; generally

---

[1] In the following notes the number of the case has reference to the Table of Cases at the end of the volume. In this table certain characteristics or noteworthy observations are inserted which give a general history of the individual case to which these notes are additions, and also proofs of the statements in the text.

I endeavor to give as nearly as possible the expressions of those who have favored me with an account of their cases. This has been done because it is to be presumed that these expressions as a general rule convey the facts most correctly, and because I thereby avoid any undue influence from my own views as to the course and nature of the disease.

Many persons doubt whether any disease like that which is the subject of this essay, really exists ; they consider it an ordinary cold, such as might occur at any season of the year. A full detail of the symptoms from sources beyond question and in sufficient number, will be likely to remove this doubt.

Case 2. Rev. H. W. Beecher. — "My nose is exquisitely sensitive, and subject to incessant and copious defluctions. The slightest draft of air produces sneezing of the most enterprising character. To sneeze in tens and twenties, with repeats *ad libitum*, is part of my daily duty. The odor of flowers, smoke, and cinders in cars, dust, perfume, or anything ordinarily without disagreeable effects, now produce sneezing and a copious secretion of thin watery mucus. After about ten days the secretions become thicker."

The same writer in the *New York Ledger* thus graphically describes his sufferings : "The nose sympathizes. Your handkerchief suddenly becomes the most important object in life. By the next day the slightest draft of wind sets you to sneezing. It is a revelation. You never before even sus-

several follow in quick succession; they are violent and effective. The paroxysms are excited by a great variety of conditions. Dust, especially that accompanied by smoke, as in a railway train, is particularly provocative of sneezes. The dust of a carpet, or from the street, are also efficient. A slight draught of air, hardly observable at the time; the change from shade to sunshine, or even the change of the body from the sitting to the upright position, will be followed by a succession of these annoyances.

The sneezing is accompanied by a greater or less discharge from the nostrils. In the early stages, this discharge is a perfectly limpid water. The quantity is often excessive, requiring in some cases the use of two or three dozen handkerchiefs daily, and yet so clear as hardly to leave a stain.[1] If the head be held down so that the blood

pected what it was really to sneeze. If the door is open, you sneeze. If a pane of glass is gone, you sneeze. If you look into the sunshine, you sneeze. If a little dust rises from the carpet, or the odor of flowers is wafted to you, or smell of smoke, you incontinently sneeze. If you sneeze once you sneeze twenty times. It is a riot of sneezes. First, a single one like a leader in a flock of sheep, bolts over; and then, in spite of all you can do, the whole flock, fifty by count, come dashing over, in twos, in fives, in bunches of twenty."

Case 22. Samuel Batchelder, Esq. — " These attacks commence after the heats of summer near the last of August, giving the impression that they are a consequence of the debility occasioned by these heats. The most prominent symptom, nasal catarrh, is manifestly increased by exposure to the dust; sometimes a slight change of temperature, either from heat to cold or from cold to heat, will produce rapid and violent sneezing. Attacks of sneezing are brought on by changing from shade to sunshine, or smelling of the milk-weed [*Asclepias cornuti*]. Sitting quietly in my office the troublesome symptoms are quiet, but getting up and moving about or going into the street, will produce a paroxysm. "

[1] *Case* 66. — " The flow from the nostrils is so profuse that three dozen handkerchiefs are used daily. There is fever, a hot dry skin, dry mouth, eyes red and watering, which continues till frost. In a week or ten days from the commencement, a cough comes on which continues till winter. She is obliged frequently to sit up at night with obstructed nostrils and asthma."

Case 36. Henry G. Fay, Esq. — "August 20th I began to sneeze and have the watery discharges from the head. This discharge commences lightly, but before the close of the season it often saturates six or eight

in it is in any degree increased, the flow is augmented, and drops follow in quick succession.

After a paroxysm of sneezing, and a flow of water from the nostrils, they become less obstructed, and sometimes quite free, and so remain for an hour or more.

These attacks are produced by the irritative causes above described; but there are also certain hours at which they are naturally most severe. The most common time for a severe fit is the early morning on first rising, when the position of the body is changed, and at the same time is exposed to a different temperature. Individuals have named certain hours of the day and night when these regular paroxysms occur, and from which they vary but little. With others they come on suddenly, irregularly, and without obvious cause.[1] They are not to be resisted or put off, like ordinary sneezing, by pressing upon the nose at its root, or other devices; they seem to have other and more powerful incentives than occur in any ordinary catarrh.

Another and not less striking characteristic is the suddenness with which they come upon the sufferer, and equal suddenness with which the whole attack disappears; they come and go off, when they do go, in a moment.

The obstruction of the nostrils is variable, and in the early stages (at times) it ceases entirely; but as the disease advances it is more complete, more constant, and at night becomes very annoying. The nostrils may be entirely closed at the same time that the flow from them continues. This state of things compels breathing through the mouth, making the tongue dry and hard; and the dry-

---

handkerchiefs *per diem.* 'This water has no color; a handkerchief may be 'sopping wet' and yet look clean. Sometimes when I stoop over with my head towards the floor, the discharge will run out of my nose like water from a pitcher almost."

[1] *Case* 15. Edward Wyman, Esq. — "The sneezing paroxysms are most severe between 11 o'clock and 12 o'clock at noon, and are accompanied by a sense of tension over the eyes. The disease is apparently more severe on alternate days."

ness and hardness not unfrequently extends to the throat, and the sleeper is aroused with a stiffness in these parts, producing a sense of suffocation.

The act of swallowing is interfered with, not only by the obstruction of the nostrils, which prevents the proper application of the palate to the posterior nares, but also, it would seem, by some nervous disturbance, by which the proper consent of action among the muscles is prevented. This is most frequently noticed in the morning at breakfast.[1] Still, however great this trouble may be, it can generally be relieved for the time by muscular exercise, — running up-stairs, leaping, or anything that promotes perspiration. By this means the obstruction of the nostrils is removed, and a large part of the difficulty at once ceases. The senses of taste and smell are much impaired, and sometimes lost.[2]

[1] *Case* 1. — "My attack begins August 20, or within a day or two of that date, with a slight stuffing of the nostrils, and in a week I begin to sneeze in paroxysms, principally in the morning on first getting up, so that sometimes it takes me more than an hour to get into condition to permit of my attempting to eat. I am also subject to paroxysms in the evening, apparently caused by the night air, and sometimes at other hours in the day. By a fortnight my eyes are greatly inflamed and my throat very sore. These symptoms continue about a fortnight, with very little abatement. Then the bronchial tubes and lungs begin to be affected, and the symptoms in the head grow less severe."

Case 10. — The obstruction of the nostrils is usually greatest on first rising or soon after, and also after a nap during the day. In the morning it frequently goes to the extent of interfering with the act of deglutition, and the movements of the uvula, producing a general disturbance in the coördination of the muscles engaged in this act, often to the extent of preventing the morsel from being swallowed and endangering choking."

Case 62. — "The obstruction of the nostrils is much relieved by exercise or going up-stairs."

[2] *Case* 10. — The sense of smell is very soon diminished, and, before the end of the first week of the disease, is, in many cases, abolished, especially during the obstructed condition of the nostrils. See, also, Case 18. The sense of taste is diminished early in the disease and the mouth becomes dry and sticky.

Case 15. "Edward Wyman, Esq. — "The nostrils become completely

Such is the state of things during the first and second weeks. After this the discharge from the nostrils diminishes and is less limpid, the obstructions less frequent, and of shorter duration. Still, the violent and prolonged sneezing continues, and the sense of taste and smell are impaired, even after the cough makes its appearance.

At this period there is added in many cases a peculiar nervous condition, which is closely connected with these affections of the head. It shows itself especially in the night, when the sufferer awakes after troubled dreams with a sense of suffocation, and an almost irresistible desire to get up and walk about, and go into the open air. This is not connected with asthma or difficult breathing, so far as the chest is concerned ; it is, apparently, a disordered nervous condition.[1]

As the disease approaches its end, during the latter part of the third and beginning of the fourth week, the nasal troubles gradually diminish and disappear with the other symptoms, leaving, however, not unfrequently a certain degree of irritability of the lining membrane, often accompanied by slight ulceration or denudations of the surface, which are sore, and painful, and bleeding.[2] In other cases the repeated annual recurrence produces a thickening of the mucous membrane which becomes permanent.[3]

obstructed; usually one at a time, but sometimes both at once, which materially interferes with deglutition. Smell and taste are then both lost."

Case 22. — "The sense of smell of late has much diminished, but the sense of taste is pretty good."

[1] *Case* 11. Mr. E. F. Atkins. — "The nostrils become so much obstructed at night as to produce a sense of difficulty in respiration, and a nervousness difficult to describe."

Case 10. — This nervousness at night, is in some stages of the disease almost uncontrollable. The sense of impending suffocation on awakening in the night, apparently on account of the obstruction of the nostrils, the dryness or stiffness of the throat, are to the sufferer for the time being truly alarming.

[2] *Case* 62. — "I have headache and pain in the eyes, not unfrequently accompanied by a bloody discharge from the nostrils."

[3] *Case* 57. Dr. Anson Hooker's case. — "She has had so much of the

THE EYES.

§ 7. The eyes are affected nearly simultaneously with the irritation of the nasal mucous membrane. The itching commences at the inner canthi, and extends over the conjunctival covering of the whole ball, and also, in a greater or less degree, to that lining the eyelids. It is at first slight and yields to a little pressure upon the lids, but as the disease advances it increases, with an intense desire to rub them.[1]

Together with the itching there is redness and swelling of the inner corners of the eye. This redness extends over the membrane, and is occasioned by the enlargement and inosculation in all directions of the conjunctival vessels. The sclerotic coat, over which the vessels can be freely moved, is not inflamed nor the vessels enlarged. At the same time there is profuse lachrymation, the tears finding their way into the nostrils, add to the discharge, already abundant, or flowing over the cheek, irritate the skin.

The itching of the eyes, like that of the nostrils, comes on suddenly and is produced by similar causes. The sensitiveness to light of the whole organ is striking; so great, that frequently the sufferer is obliged to shut himself up

catarrhal inflammation that the mucous membrane of the nostrils is permanently thickened, obstructing them to such an extent as to oblige her to breathe through the mouth."

Case 67. — Has gradually increasing and more permanent thickening of the nasal mucous membrane, impeding respiration, and producing partial deafness.

[1] *Case* 18. — Suffers so much from the itching of the eyes that he cannot resist rubbing them, thereby increasing the irritation ; he is often obliged to tie down his hands before going to sleep to protect his eyes from injury.

Case 57. Dr. Anson Hooker's case. — The eyes are first affected, then the nose, throat, ears, and bronchia. The itching of the eyes is intolerable and very much aggravated by rubbing, blowing the nose, talking, singing, or much exercise. There is a profuse running secretion from the nostrils, and considerable mucous discharge from the throat and lungs.

in a dark room,[1] or use his eyes but an hour or two daily.[2]

The attacks are sudden and often without obvious cause; but they usually accompany, or follow closely, those of the nose. The itching and lachrymation once commenced, the irresistible desire to rub them follows, and under the pressure and rubbing, the vessels enlarge, and the whole surface is soon of an almost uniform vermilion color. This enlargement of the vessels gives a sensation of roughness in the eye, but it is far less annoying than the itching which precedes it.

Notwithstanding this apparently serious state of things, the lachrymation and intense redness disappear usually within twenty or thirty minutes, and leave the eye often but slightly worse for the attack; a succession of symptoms quite unlike those of ordinary ophthalmia.[3]

---

[1] *Case* 46. — Franklin Hunt, Esq., says: "The itching of the eyes is very severe; I cannot resist rubbing them violently, and am obliged to remain in a dark room, with the eyes covered, three or four days at a time."

Case 24. — "The eyes are so sensitive to light that I am obliged to confine myself for days in succession to a darkened room."

[2] Daniel Webster. "I use the confidential hand of another to write you a short letter, my eyes holding out only to perform a small part of the duty expected of them every day. I am in the midst of my periodical catarrh, or 'Hay Fever,' or whatever you please to call it. I read nothing, and hardly write anything but signatures." And again, "my eyes allow me to write only about an hour a day." — *Private Correspondence*, vol. ii. p. 385.

"*Marshfield, Sept.* 12, 1852. When the sun is very bright, I am obliged to avoid going out, on account of my eyes, except indeed when the sea is calm, and I am protected by an awning." — *Private Correspondence*, vol. ii. p. 552.

[3] I have never seen any allusion to this affection of the eyes in any special treatise. It certainly does not correspond with what is termed catarrhal ophthalmia. The course of the disease, and its disappearance without treatment, as the primary affection disappears, gives it a peculiar character worthy of a place in systematic works upon the diseases of these organs.

Case 80. — Mrs. F., during an attack applied to an eminent oculist in New York, who diagnosticated *granular conjunctivitis*, and treated her with nitrate of silver; after three visits, finding herself much worse for the application, she abandoned the treatment, and her eyes gradually recovered as the critical period passed by.

There is a sense of fullness over the eyes;[1] the eyelids are swollen, the lower one most, and often œdematous, especially in the morning on first rising.[2]

The edges of the lids are inflamed, and the secretion of the meibomian glands is increased and apparently irritating. Crusts form upon their orifices, and hence, not unfrequently, small ulcers beneath them. Sties are by no means an uncommon accompaniment of these difficulties.[3] These troubles do not usually make their appearance until the second or third week.

The lachrymal secretion diminishes in quantity, but becomes thicker, as the disease advances, and the lids are frequently glued together in the morning. In the night, the attempt to open the eye is attended with a spasmodic closing of the lids and a sensation of sticks and sand under them, which is only relieved by the free lachrymation which follows. As a general rule, both eyes suffer equally and at the same time.

By the end of the third week the affection has nearly ceased, and in a short time the whole trouble disappears without permanent disability in the organs.

THE MOUTH AND THROAT.

§ 8. These passages are affected in the early stages. The mucous membrane is reddened and thickened. There is itching of the roof of the mouth and the parts beyond. The velum is relaxed and thickened, and the uvula often so much elongated and swollen, that it gives the sensation of

---

[1] *Case* 56. — Has a sense of fullness over the eyes.

[2] Rev. H. W. Beecher. — "My eyes puff out and are very sensitive to the light, and full of tears. This stage lasts about a week or ten days, my eyes growing worse and the light more intolerable. A walk of half an hour in the full sunlight, is enough at any time to bring on a paroxysm of eye symptoms. After about ten days the secretions become thicker, the nose is stuffed, the *eye* grows stronger, but the *lids* are inflamed and itch incessantly. About the fourth week the eyes are quite well."

[3] *Case* 66. — The eyes become very much inflamed and sometimes closed, as if suffering from a sty.

a foreign body hanging there ;[1] and falling backward toward the throat, compels to frequent hawking to throw it forward upon the tongue.   This swelling and stiffness, combined with the inability to breathe through the nostrils, occasions the difficulty of swallowing, so much insisted upon by the sufferers.[2]

The tonsils are swollen and painful, especially in swallowing.   The secretions are thickened and sticky.

The itching just mentioned extends to the posterior nares, and also through the eustachian tube to the ears. It is so annoying that the tongue is frequently applied to all parts of the mouth within its reach, and rubbed against them for temporary relief.[3]   It also occasions frequent hawking and other acts which give motion to the parts. The itching of the ears is as intolerable as the attempts at relief by thrusting the fingers into the external passage are unsuccessful.   The lining membrane of this passage is frequently irritated, and discharges a thin, limpid fluid.[4]

On inspection of the parts within the mouth, a redness and swelling is seen, with some enlargement of the mucous glands at the posterior part, but no ulcerations of the surface, nor any tendency to diptheritic deposits.

[1] *Case* 10. Author. — The sensation in the throat is of a general swelling and confusion of the parts ; an indefiniteness as to the position of organs, producing distress as to swallowing, more annoying than can well be described.   The closed nostrils and consequent breathing through the mouth during sleep make it and the throat dry and almost immovable, arousing the sleeper with a sense of impending suffocation.

[2] Rev. Henry Ward Beecher. — " Eating becomes a matter of skill.   You cannot eat with your mouth at the same time that you are breathing through it.   Two trains meeting on a single track, one or the other must switch off.   Thus, you chew and hold your breath ; and then you switch to one side your cud, and breathe a while.   Thus you shut off, alternately, bread and breath.   This stage lasts about two weeks more."

[3] *Case* 59. — " I have almost constant tickling of the roof of the mouth and throat, varying in severity but continuing through the period of attack. The trouble in the throat, as a general rule, is worse in the night."

[4] This secretion may sometimes be produced by the irritation following attempts to relieve the itching, but in others it appears without any such cause.   It seems to be one of the consequences of the general irritation of the mucous surfaces.

CHEST.

§ 9. The symptoms of the chest may be divided into two classes, cough and asthma.

Cough. Although very few escape cough in some form, it is not so constant a symptom as those already described.[1] It commences at the end of the first week with a tickling at the top of the windpipe, producing a frequent short cough — a cough of irritation.[2] The tickling soon becomes more constant and the cough more annoying, with pain behind the breast-bone and some soreness of the throat. This pain is especially severe in the morning on first awaking, when it has a tearing character.

By the end of the second week the cough becomes paroxysmal, and although it often occurs together with the attacks of sneezing and nose-blowing, and keeps pace with these in a degree, it also comes on at other times and from other causes. The night attacks are severe, painful, and so incessant that no sleep can be got for hours together. The patient is often obliged to sit up in bed, leaning forward and grasping his knees, or, leaving his bed altogether, as he becomes fatigued, he grasps firm objects to aid in the spasmodic efforts for relief.[3] The expectoration is little or nothing at this stage. Often, after a long succession of

---

[1] *Case* 7. Dr. J. C. Hayden. — "I have no cough, excepting sufficient to dislodge a somewhat increased secretion from the lungs."

Case 59. Mrs. B. — "The cough commences in the last two weeks, but it is not a constant symptom, nor does it become very annoying. There is very little expectoration."

[2] *Case* 3. John J. Dixwell, Esq. — "Early in September a bronchial affection sets in, when the nasal catarrh has diminished, and continues through the month, and sometimes through the whole winter."

[3] *Case* 60. Dr. Derby's case. — "After about two weeks, irritation commences in the throat with cough; at first slight and not very frequent, and without expectoration. This cough increases, and during the last two weeks becomes extremely annoying and almost incessant while lying down, compelling her to sleep in an almost upright position. She first suffered from asthma in September, 1864, four months before the birth of her first child."

coughs, a very ˙˙ ᵘ transparent mucus, stringy and tough, is thrown off, giving only slight momentary relief.[1] These attacks cease, like the attacks of sneezing, apparently when the nervous system is fatigued and thus exhausted of its excessive irritability. It is at this period that the violence of the cough often produces retching,[2] which sometimes ends in vomiting.[3]

By the end of the second week or the middle of the third, the cough is less irritating and seems deeper in the chest. At this time it is often accompanied by pains at the lower parts of the chest, around the points where the muscles exercised in these violent efforts are attached. There is a slight wheezing or whistling during expiration principally, not impeding respiration but making it somewhat noisy.

The expectoration is thicker, starch-like, in larger quantity, and its expulsion gives a certain degree of relief to the cough.[4] It is generally yellowish, sometimes greenish, and only occasionally streaked with blood.

The ordinary termination is at the end of the fourth week; at other times, and with some individuals habitually, it takes its leave very gradually, or even extends into the winter.

§ 10. *Asthma.* This sets in generally about the fourth

---

[1] *Case* 20. W. H. Y. Hackett, Esq., of Portsmouth, N. H. — "The greatest severity is during the first three weeks, and of these the second is the most severe. It goes off with a hard cough and a difficulty in raising mucus. In the night it often takes the form of asthma, rendering it difficult to sleep."

[2] *Case* 62. — "Cough often spasmodic, producing retching and a disposition to vomit, but not absolute vomiting."

[3] *Case* 22. — "At times, especially in the night, the cough is very severe, spasmodic in character, and in some instances producing vomiting."

[4] Rev. Henry Ward Beecher. — "About the fourth week the eyes are entirely well, the nose somewhat congested still, but the disease drops down upon the chest. Asthma develops. A convulsive cough sets in. In the morning I raise a thick, starch-like mucus, without blood or any admixture, but like calf's-foot jelly. It has a slight metallic taste. This stage lasts about a week or ten days."

week, after the cough has lost something of its severity, and the watering of the eyes, the sneezing, and discharge from the nose diminished.[1]   With some it begins at the end of the first week.[2]   It is by no means so constant a symptom as these, nor is it so constant as the cough.[3] Many escape it altogether, and to those who do not escape it, it is generally much less annoying than the earlier symptoms.   The attacks of difficult breathing may be severe, but they are not as long as those arising from other causes.[4] They usually come on during the night, after the first sleep, and cease in about an hour, to reappear towards morning.[5]

[1] *Case* 4. — "I have never had asthma at any other time except once when I was very much exposed and wet.   The asthma is severe at times, particularly after eating heartily, when it is much worse.   When I am suffering from asthma I am generally free from either running or irritation at the eyes or nose.   It lasts till the latter part of September; [this is in Philadelphia, Penn.;] by the 1st of October I am perfectly free from the cold proper; though sometimes for a year or two past, by not taking proper care of myself when it was passing away, I have had a cough for sometime afterwards, generally a slight one, but still annoying.   Sensitiveness of the nose and eyes of late years has increased."

[2] *Case* 9.   Robert F. Fiske, Esq., of St. Paul, Minnesota. — "My autumn cold while I lived at the east [New England] was very punctual in its advent about the 20th of August.   The mucous membrane of all the air passages in time became very much inflamed.   For many nights after the 1st of September, to about the 12th, I was unable to get any comfortable sleep, because of the severe attacks of asthma which were always a part of the affliction occasioned by the cold, and generally every afternoon I was mentally and physically prostrated by a hot, dry, burning fever."

[3] *Case* 57.   Dr. Anson Hooker's case. — "At times has asthmatic attacks, the feeling of breathing through gauze or sponge."

Case 1. — "Sometimes I have an asthmatic attack, but by no means every year.   During three years only have I had difficult breathing."

[4] *Case* 42. — Dr. P. suffered severely from asthma, beginning at the end of the first week, and ending with the complaint about the first of October. With him it was by far the most distressing part of the disease.

[5] *Case* 8.   Daniel Webster. — "Sometimes the force of the catarrh seems pretty much broken, and then it returns, attacking the head, eyes, nose, etc., with great violence.   I think it is approaching its last stage, which is the asthmatic stage.   Some of our friends, who are subjects of the complaint, and who have short necks, dread this.   I do not fear much from this, although in this stage I feel its influence more or less on the chest." — *Private Correspondence, Sept.* 28, 1851.

Some accuse a hearty meal as the cause, but with most the paroxysm is without obvious cause.

Examination by auscultation and percussion furnishes no other signs than those of an ordinary catarrh. Mucous râles are heard, and in some parts of the chest there is deficiency of respiratory sound ; the asthma is accompanied by sibilant râles, and the noisy inspiration and expiration common with this affection. Percussion is natural.

The absence of bronchitis, or other affections of the lungs or of the heart ; the suddenness with which the attacks begin and end, lead to the belief that they are in part, at least, spasmodic, and not dependent upon organic lesion. That the larger bronchiæ, and those of the second order, have muscular fibres, is proved ; and we have no right to deny to these passages the possibility of spasm, when no one denies it to similar fibres in the stomach, intestines, bladder, and other hollow organs. With regard to the minute bronchiæ and air vesicles, it is not improbable that their vessels may undergo changes similar to those in the nostrils and conjunctiva, by which these passages are temporarily shut, and, like them, as suddenly opened. In all phases of this singular disease the nervous element is strongly marked.[1]

HEART.

§ 11. The action of the heart is more frequent and its beats quicker than in health.[2] During the latter stages

---

[1] Trousseau describes cases of persons who suffer at various seasons of the year for two or three months, from attacks of sneezing and watering of the eyes, repeated three or four times daily. In the interval they are perfectly well, and yet, without evidence of disease in the respiratory system, sooner or later develop asthma. The two affections he considers expressions of the same nervous disorder. — Trousseau, *Clinique Medicale*, vol. ii. p. 442, Paris, 1868.

[2] *Case* 27. — "By the end of the fourth week in September, the lungs suffer, and asthmatic breathing sets in ; the attacks at times severe with a good deal of cough during the intervals of the paroxysms. The action of the heart is at the same time increased. Soon after the middle of September, all the symptoms abate, and disappear during the last week of the same month."

the pulse is not unfrequently intermittent, with a peculiar
uncomfortable feeling in the left breast, as though the respiration were in some way interfered with.[1]   There is
also shortness of breath on exertion, especially in ascending heights.[2]   Generally this condition of the heart is
temporary, and ends with the other symptoms.   In other
cases it has continued longer, and some have dated heart
trouble from an attack of Autumnal Catarrh.[3]

SKIN.

§ 12.   The skin does not escape the influence of the
disease.   In some cases itching of the scalp is one of the
first symptoms, accompanying the watering of the eyes,
and the discharge from the nose.   More frequently it appears in the later stages ;[4]   then the trouble is upon the

[1] *Case* 10. Author. — After having suffered from catarrh for many
years, I perceived toward the later stages that my pulse was becoming
irregular in its beats, and also variable in strength, and at times intermitting. This increased with the successive attacks, and even extended
into the winter. Since my visits at the mountains during the critical
period, this symptom has disappeared entirely. I cannot but think it was
caused by the catarrh.

[2] *Case* 3. John J. Dixwell, Esq. — "I have had no asthmatic troubles,
although I have had some difficulty of breathing on going up hill, which
has increased very much during the last two or three years, caused by a
certain degree of enlargement of the heart."

[3] *Case* 28. — Judge Shaw suffered from heart disease, followed by drop-
sical effusions, of which he died. Dr. Hayward was of opinion that the
disease was aggravated, if not produced, by the Autumnal Catarrh, and the
consequent obstruction of the circulation through the lungs.

Joseph Peabody, Esq., informs me of a jurist of Chicago who suffered
from cardiac disease, which he believed was produced by Autumnal Catarrh.

[4] *Case* 71. — "Commences with itching of the scalp, followed by itching
of the eyes and nose, and a profuse discharge from the nostrils — sometimes
eight or ten handkerchiefs will be saturated with limpid water before breakfast, frequently two dozen in the course of the day."

Case 46. — "The irritation of the skin, especially of the scalp, is quite
annoying."

Case 70. — "I suffer from itching of the skin, especially on the back.

Case 66. — "Itching of general surface." This itching is of a peculiar
kind. The surface of the skin is, to the eye, perfectly well. There are
neither pimples nor redness, but the itching on the scapulæ is almost incessant. The itching of the chin and face, in my own case, is annoying, and

shoulder blades, or along the spine ; sometimes the skin over the breast-bone is the seat. Either from rubbing, to allay the intense itching, or from some other cause, small pimples appear. If the tops are removed a little serum exudes, which dries, and forms a scale.

The alæ of the nose are irritated, and small vesicles form, which may remain some days and then dry up, or the skin may be more deeply affected with slight ulcerations, lasting a week or two. With some individuals the whole nose is swollen and red, the interior of the nostrils inflamed, causing very considerable annoyance. The upper lip is chafed by the discharge from the nostrils and the use of the handkerchief, and herpetic eruptions appear around the mouth.

That the skin is in an unnatural condition is proved by the fact that it is easily chafed ; and the chafed spots, instead of soon drying up with a slight scale, pour forth serum for some days. After healing, the new cuticle remains a long time red and tender, and easily abraded. This is most frequently seen around the neck.

The axillæ are often irritated ; the glands enlarge, and small abscesses form, which are painful, and come slowly to the surface ; or, failing in this, the inflamed part long remains hard and sensitive.[1]

The tendency to perspiration on slight exertion is increased, and often the whole surface is moist and clammy. is only relieved by frequent rubbing. The itching on the shoulders is relieved only by hard rubbing with a stiff brush until smarting is produced.

[1] Rev. H. W. Beecher. — After a week or ten days of the asthma, " The disease quietly disappears, or else it breaks up with some row in the system, such as a breaking out all over the body of itching blotches, or a violent night of cough and asthma, that wrenches everything about one."

Case 44. J. T. Hodge, Esq. — "Besides extreme itching of the skin, I have been troubled with an eruption on my legs and wrists, sometimes scattered and again in bunches, which become swollen and sore. These also itch at intervals violently, and when the pustules become raw and scab over, they do not heal. I had supposed it 'prickly heat,' but as it has now come on for the third year with the 'Hay Fever,' it seems to belong to it. With the eruption on the limbs, I have little sties on the eyelids of one eye, which have lasted now over four weeks."

§ 13. BESIDES the local symptoms described in the fore-going sections, there are others of uncertain seat, which should be known, for the full understanding of the disease.

Some patients describe a stage of incubation or devel-opment, commencing a week or fortnight before the more distinct onset, during which there is a slight febrile ex-citement, easily increased by a cold, or by irregularity of diet.[1] With many there is an unusual sensitiveness of the nervous system, for a few days at least, before the at-tack.

In some cases the attack commences with weakness, a sense of exhaustion, or " goneness at the stomach,"[2] sleep unsound, and disturbed by unpleasant dreams, headache, and general uneasiness.

More frequently it is only after a few days that signs of

[1] *Case* 2. Rev. H. W. Beecher. — " There is, I am persuaded, a slight febrile disturbance of the system. Ordinarily, it is not troublesome, or even noticeable. But the least cold taken, or the slightest irregularity of diet, develops heat and a kind of knitting of the sutures of the skull, as if they were slightly moving or matching themselves over again. Sleep is also full of dreams not celestial. But the whole passes so lightly, that I did not till within three years make it a matter of study."

Daniel Webster. — " The enemy may come as a thief in the night, or he may be as bold as a lion." — *Correspondence*, vol. ii. p. 463.

" *Aug.* 29*th.* — About noon, I thought I felt catarrhal symptoms. There was some tendency of defluxion from the nose, the eyes did not feel right, and what was more important, I felt a degree of general depression, which belongs to the disease." — *Ibid.* p. 469.

[2] *Case* 40. — " The attack commences August 20, with great weakness, which is soon followed by a ' sense of goneness ' at the epigastrium, and palpitation of the heart. The weakness diminishes with the catarrhal development, and this last also diminishes with the commencement of Asthma."

constitutional disturbance appear.[1]   Chills, and heats, and burning of the palms, are among the common symptoms of fever.[2]   Often a chilliness over the whole surface, and a sensitiveness to cold, which prompts to the use of warmer clothing, at night especially.[3]   Generally there is little evidence of the third stage of fever, the sweating ; but in exceptional cases the sweating towards the end of the disease is profuse and exhausting.[4]

The pulse is generally accelerated and weakened.   The action of the heart is weakened, and easily accelerated by slight exertion ; its sounds are shorter and more abrupt than in health.   There is palpitation.

[1] In 1866 Morrill Wyman, Jr. (Case 14) while under the influence of the catarrh, left Cambridge, September 7, for the White Mountains.   He suffered much in the railway train, but in the afternoon bore very well the fatigue of ascending Grand Monadnock, 3,718 feet.   The following day, late in the evening, he reached the Crawford House.   His feet and hands were cold, he coughed much and slept little.   9th. Pulse 100 ; tongue coated ; appetite slight ; too weak to walk out of doors without great fatigue ; head ache and giddiness.   During the night his skin was flushed, hot and dry.   On the 10th he reached the Glen by the way of Upper Bart-lett.   In two or three days all these symptoms disappeared, and he remained well during his stay at the mountains.

[2] Case 20. W. H. Y. Hackett, Esq. — " I have the symptoms of fever, high pulse, hot palms, and severe pressure upon the lungs.   For a month I am unfit for my business.   I am a lawyer, and have on several occasions had to give over the trial of a case after it was opened.   Its greatest severity is in the first three weeks, the most severe is the second.   It goes off with a hard cough with a difficulty in raising mucus.   In the night it often takes the form of asthma, rendering it difficult to sleep."

In my own case there is heat and feverishness, perhaps more thirst than usual ; but the disease with me displays its constitutional influence rather in general uneasiness, and a sensitiveness to a fall of temperature.

[3] Dr. Derby's case. — " The influence upon the system shows itself in a loss of strength, loss of appetite, and loss of flesh ; a sense of chilliness of the whole body, which prompts her to use more clothing than most persons, especially at night."

[4] Case 43. — " My general health is less firm than formerly, and I have a bronchitis which extends into the winter with nasal catarrh.   I have profuse night sweats through the height of the disease, which at first give some relief, but when further advanced, prove exhausting."

The strength is decidedly lessened;[1] and, in addition, a disinclination to exertion which is hardly to be attributed to this weakness; it is out of proportion to it ; it is rather a want of will to make effort of any kind.

The appetite is generally diminished, but not much thirst;[2] there is loss of flesh, sometimes rapid and considerable, even when the symptoms are not severe. The cessation of the symptoms is accompanied by as rapid a recovery of the usual weight.

The condition of the bowels is subject to variation as to constipation, or the reverse, during the attack, but there is no evidence that it bears any close relation to it. In two cases an attack of cholera morbus, or some similar affection of the bowels, occurred at the time when Autumnal Catarrh usually appeared ; in both cases the catarrh came on a week later. " Typhoid fever and dysentery " are reported to have replaced the disease.[3]

---

[1] *Case 32.*— "I lose strength and am so much prostrated generally that I am unable to walk about. The loss of appetite is as complete as though I was suffering from acute fever. My disease has sometimes, so far as the cough is concerned, followed me into the winter, so also has the expectoration of mucus." Mr. W. of Brandon, lost flesh, and the cough continued so long into the winter as to become alarming. He has been in Quebec in 1870, perfectly well during the catarrhal season.

Case 66. — " There is always much fever, constant flashes of heat passing over the whole body, hands very dry and hot. It is impossible to tell you of the great lassitude which accompanies it."

[2] *Case* 20. W. H. Y. Hackett, Esq. — "Except a few days when sickest, I have a good appetite, better than at other times. But my strength is very much reduced. The second week of the attack I am most of the time unable to sit up, and can take but little food."

Case 59. — "Appetite and strength diminish during the progress of the disease, compelling her to keep her bed a part of the time."

Case 38. — Was at the Glen House August 12th. Previous to that time had been losing flesh. October 1st he left the Glen, on his return home on the Hudson one hundred and twenty miles from its mouth ; he had gained in weight one half pound daily. August 26, 1868, he had lost twenty-five pounds of flesh, and was much weakened, but had not felt sick. He suffers from palpitation of the heart during the attack.

[3] *Case* 66. — " I have given you ' Hay Fever ' as I have it every season, but this season my experience has been very different. The third week in

That the impression upon the nervous system is decided, must be admitted. The greater part of the sufferers speak of the discouraging, depressing effects, and utter inability to do mental work, in the after part of the day especially. The feeling that there is no escape until the customary period has passed, weighs heavily upon them.[1] This,

August (the time of the usual attack of catarrh) I was attacked very severely with *cholera morbus;* for three days was severely ill; did not entirely recover until the first of September; then the Hay Fever came on (before my illness I had all the symptoms of the disease); when it did come the sneezing was only a short time, but the asthma worse than I ever had it. The cough very hard, tight; I could not speak without coughing; breathing very short, so I could not walk across the room without suffering for breath. I have heard of a person who had catarrh many years; one year she did not have it and was very dangerously ill with typhoid fever and dysentery, the next year the Hay Fever came back again. I do believe it is a protection against other diseases."

Case 45. C. F. W. — One year had an affection of the bowels with diarrhœa; the catarrh did not appear until this ceased, when it came on as severely as ever.

[1] *Case* 8. Daniel Webster. — " The disease is depressing and discouraging. I know that there is no remedy for it, and that it must have its course. It produces loss of appetite and great loss of strength."

The following letter from Mr. Webster to President Fillmore indicates the severity of the disease and its depressing influence : —

" *Boston, November* 5, 1850. — I left New Hampshire yesterday, having become free of disease, and well, except so far as this protracted catarrh has reduced me. I am quite aware how inconvenient my long absence is to you and to the government, and sometimes feel that as this illness is of annual recurrence, I ought to regard it as unfitting me for an office [Secretary of State], the duties of which require constant attention. I must now go to Marshfield for a few days." *Private Correspondence,* vol. ii. p. 400.

" *Washington, September* 10, 1820. — My annual cold is now heavy upon me, weakening my body and depressing my spirits. It has yet a fortnight to run, and perhaps will sink me lower than it did when strong excitement enabled me to withstand it. I have lost a good deal of flesh, and you will think me thin and haggard. My eyes allow me to write only about an hour a day." " *September* 12. I am in the midst of my periodical catarrh or 'Hay Fever,' or whatever you please to call it. I read nothing, and hardly write anything but signatures."

" *Marshfield, October* 3, 1851. The catarrh with its sneezing and nose-blowing, its cough and its asthma seems to be taking leave ; my eyes are still weak, but my greatest difficulty at present is a general want of strength."

however, is not universal; some declare that with the exception of the eyes, or the annoyance from the obstruction of the nostrils, and nose-blowing, the readiness for intellectual labor is as great as ever.[1]

Fullness and heaviness of the head, painful sensations in the forehead and behind the ears, and a painful feeling as of a band around the head above the eyes; partial deafness; are not unfrequent symptoms in some stage of the affection.[2]

The nervousness at night, and the consequent inability to sleep, are frequently complained of. If sleep is obtained, it is troubled with dreams, and a sense of suffocation, not always dispelled on awaking.[3] These sensations may occur without any of the symptoms of asthma, either in difficult breathing or wheezing. During the day, also, there are nervous sensations of a different kind, — irritability, and liability to annoyance from trifles.

The disease is peculiar in its variations in severity from day to day. At times, the relief for the most of the day will be so great, that in spite of many former disappointments the patient is persuaded that his troubles have now come to an end. A single symptom, like asthma, will be relieved, and the only annoyance will be from the nose

---

[1] *Case 9.* — "Generally every afternoon I was mentally and physically prostrated by a hot, dry, burning fever."

Rev. H. W. Beecher. — "Otherwise than the difficulty of using the eyes, there is no hindrance to intellectual labor."

[2] *Case 19.* — "I have a pain in the forehead and behind the ears."

Case 58. — Has a sense of fullness in the head, with pain, and a feeling as of a band around the head above the eyes.

Case 39. — "I have pain in the head and partial deafness."

[3] *Case 10.* Author. — I have at night suffered much from a peculiar nervousness difficult to describe, but which prevents sleep and almost drives me from my bed to relieve a sense of closeness in the air for which I know there is no reason. There is also an irritability during the day which is unknown at other times, and which often makes my duties irksome. The accompanying weakness during the third week adds very materially to these troubles.

Case 69. — "The disease is accompanied by a nervous, irritable state."

and eyes.   And yet on the following day the more painful symptoms will return with all their force.[1] This has
probably given rise to the belief, with some, in its intermittent character.[2] If there is any intermission on alternate days, it is so rare that it can hardly be held to be a
characteristic of the disease.

It is not a little singular that by far the greater number
of persons who have undergone these annual attacks do
not find that the health has suffered. As a general rule, the
weakness and discouragement disappear, and the various
organs show but little evidence of the recent disturbance.[3]
Indeed, some declare that they enjoy better health after
the attack than before it.[4]

Again, the subjects of the disease are not subjects of
catarrhal affections at other seasons of the year more than
persons generally. Some declare that they are less subject to them, that they very rarely have colds from exposures that are likely to produce them in others.[5]

---

[1] *Case* 8.   Daniel Webster. — "Some days I feel quite well, and can
keep out without inconvenience if the weather be fair; on other days I cannot go out at all, fair or foul."

Case 2.   Rev. H. W. Beecher. — "During the whole period of from five
to six weeks, the disease is subject to distinct remissions. Although I have
had twenty years' experience, I am not cured of believing, every year, that
it has ended its career two or three times during its progress."

[2] *Case* 15.   Edward Wyman, Esq. — "I think I have observed an intermitting character in the symptoms; that they were more severe on alternate
days."

[3] *Case* 22.   Samuel Batchelder, Esq. — Was first attacked at the age
of 24, and has experienced an attack each year from that time till 1871.
He is now 87, and is hale and active. The severity of the attack has not
increased, perhaps rather diminished within the past few years.

[4] *Case* 20.   W. H. Y. Hackett, Esq. — "I have never perceived that my
general health was affected by the 'Hay Fever,' and I am generally in better
health after the attack is over than before it came on. I dread the approach
of the middle of August, as the certain approach of suffering."

[5] *Case* 27. — Is well through the other seasons of the year; he never
suffers from catarrh in June, nor at other times from ordinary cold more
if as much as most persons.

Case 15.   Edward Wyman, Esq. — Has suffered from annual catarrh in
September, for twenty-eight years in succession. He has no catarrhal

In several instances those who have suffered from a catarrh in June, — "Rose Cold," "Hay Fever," — and have subsequently had a regularly recurring catarrh in autumn, have at once ceased to suffer from the first, or have, at least, found it much mitigated in severity.   In other cases two successive catarrhs have appeared at each of the seasons, and after a few returns the first cease.   In all cases the Autumnal Catarrh is the more severe.[1]

In but three instances has pneumonia been noted as occurring in the course of the disease.   In one case, a recurrence of the pneumonia three or four years in succession, during the attack of catarrh, is reported.   This succession would lead to a question of diagnosis, especially as it can-

symptoms annually recurring in June, and seldom has a cold at other times of the year.

Case 1. — "I ought to state that I think the 'cold' is a disease attacking the whole system, and attended with a good deal of fever; certainly it often makes me very sick, used up, and good for nothing; but on the other hand, I never suffer from colds, or very rarely, and enjoy good health, having never been sick before this malarial fever caught on the bar of the Mississippi River."

Case 69. — Has very seldom a cold at any other season of the year, never like that of September.

[1] *Case* 58. — First experienced a cold (hay cold) in June when sixteen years old, while walking in a garden in New Bedford, Mass.   Her first attack of Autumnal Catarrh was when she was thirty-four, at Fitchburg, Mass.   From that time it has recurred annually, and the June Cold has very much diminished.   She never had cough with the June Cold, with the Autumnal it is severe.

Case 75. — Mrs. Bancroft, Delaware County, Pennsylvania, from twelve years of age has had June Cold, beginning June 20th to 30th.   The paroxysm came on with great regularity at 2 A. M., 4 A. M., 8 A. M., 12 M., 4 P. M., and at bedtime, each attack lasting an hour.   It ceases the first week in July. 1861–1865 lived in Washington, and had no attack of June Cold.   The affection is of the eyes and nose alone; no trouble in the throat or lungs, no loss of appetite, no prostration.   After the cessation of the June Cold, Autumnal Catarrh came on with severe asthma.   The attack commenced annually August 19th or 20th.

Case 41.   J. W. Danforth, Esq. — Had an annual catarrh, which for three or four years commenced in June, while roses were in bloom.   The attack at this season of the year ceased when the Autumnal Catarrh commenced; this last has continued to the present time, about nineteen years.

not be verified by a detailed history of the symptoms. In one instance, the pneumonia appeared in September; the catarrh ceased for two weeks to return after the pneumonia disappeared.[1]

It must be admitted that however rapidly most patients recover perfect health after an attack, some evidently fall into bronchitis, and so continue with cough and expectoration through the autumn and even into the winter. In one case, the disease became alarming, and a removal to Georgia through the winter was thought advisable. Under the influence of the mild climate it disappeared.

The fact that Autumnal Catarrh does not prepare the way for an inroad of inflammatory diseases of the chest to the extent that the violence of the symptoms would lead us to expect, makes against its supposed inflammatory character.

§ 14. By an examination of the table of cases at the end of the volume, it will be seen that the groups of symptoms vary in severity and in constancy. With these changes and combinations, the disease assumes different external appearances. The expressions of disease in an individual suffering from asthma are very different from those of one who suffers from head symptoms only, or from cough. So, again, it may be of longer or shorter duration, varying in

---

[1] *Case* 64. — In 1856 had pneumonia in the month of September, while suffering from catarrh. Was ill two weeks, during which the catarrh was suspended, to return after the pneumonia ceased. After this had the first attack of asthma.

Case 19. — "In 1865, during second week in September, I was attacked with chills, followed by fever and headache, cough, expectoration of brick-dust color, and very adhesive. I was kept in bed two weeks, and did not recover strength under seven weeks." Although he is unable to state the diagnosis, there is good reason for believing that he suffered from an attack of pneumonia.

Case 75. Mrs. S. B. — "In 1864 I had pneumonia. I have asthmatic attacks which occur at any part of the year, but they are most severe in September. My nostrils are so much obstructed that I am unable to swallow."

the time of its annual appearance, or disappearance, or both. In this manner only can we speak of it as having different forms. We have none of those distinctions which are important in diagnosis or prognosis, that we see in pneumonia, or typhoid or intermittent fever.

The following abstract of the table at the end of the volume exhibits the different groups of symptoms and their relations to the sexes so far as stated : —

		Head Symptoms. (Eyes, Ears, Nose, Throat.)	Chest Symptoms.	
			Cough.	Asthma.
Severe .	Males . . .	45	18	16
	Females . .	20	13	10
Mild . .	Males . . .	6	22	8
	Females . .	3	7	3
Slight, or	Males . . .	3	12	28
Wanting	Females . .	3	5	11
		80	77	76

An examination of this abstract shows at once the great preponderance of the affections of the eyes, ears, nose, and throat over the other groups. In one instance only were these affections wanting ; and in a large number the severity greatly exceeded that of the other groups. Next to these stands the cough. Of the fifty-three males, only eleven escaped or had it slightly, and of the twenty-five females, five escaped. The cases of severe asthma are nearly equal to those of severe cough, but there is quite a large number — twenty-five males and thirteen females — in which it is very slight or entirely wanting. The chest symptoms evidently stand in a much nearer relation to each other than they do to the head symptoms.

3

TIME OF BEGINNING, DURATION OF GROUPS OF SYMPTOMS, AND
TERMINATION OF THE DISEASE.

§ 15. The commencement is marked in various ways.
By some it is said to begin as soon as the system is debili-
tated by the heats of summer, by others the attack is first
felt on the approach of cool weather,[1] in both cases, therefore, variable.[2] Others, more definitely, note the days
within which it appears, while others, again, declare that
the symptoms begin on the same day of the month by the
calendar, for years in succession.[3] Dr. Hayward says that
Judge Shaw was attacked on the same day, and almost at
the same hour, each year.[4] Some think it is connected

[1] *Case* 73. — Second question: When does it commence ? Answer:
" The first cool nights the last of August." This patient resides in Fall
River, Mass.

[2] *Case* 22. Samuel Batchelder, Esq., of Cambridge. — "This attack
commences after the heats of summer, near the last of August, giving
the impression that it is a consequence of the debility occasioned by these
heats."

[3] *Case* 44. — "My wife and her sisters in Plymouth, Mass., have the
disease on the 28th of August, annually. If I were in Brooklyn, N. Y.,
and my wife in Plymouth, Mass., it was punctual in its visitation to each
of us and to her sister; and with all of us it lasted six or eight weeks.

Case 4. — "It commences about the 23d or 24th of August, sometimes
perhaps a day or two sooner."

Case 21. — Gave the period of invasion from the 20th August to the 5th
of September, varying with the state of the atmosphere. In a second
letter, recently received, the dates given are from about the 10th to 15th
August. "Have found that *all localities* in New England or the Provinces,
within fifty miles of the ocean, invite an attack from about the 10th to 15th
of August, whilst elevated positions inland (away from the ocean) always
mitigate the severity of the disease." This statement is undoubtedly too
sweeping.

[4] Dr. Hayward's account of the case of Lemuel Shaw, late Chief Justice of the Supreme Court of Massachusetts, states that he " had been the
subject of this affection for thirty years, and it recurred the same day, the

with vegetation, and as that is forward or late, so the attack is hastened or delayed.[1]   One sufferer declares that his disease commences as soon as the pollen appears upon the Indian corn[2] (*Zea mays*). I have noticed that it is nearly coincident with the flowering of Roman wormwood (*Ambrosia artemisiæfolia*).

An examination of the tabular view shows more variations than some of these statements would lead us to expect.

Table showing the Number attacked during each Week in August.

First week in August	1
Second week	3
Third week	50
Fourth week	17
First week in October	1
Uncertain	1
	—
	73

From this it appears that in nearly nine tenths it begins

18th of August, and almost at the same hour." Lemuel Shaw, Esq., of Boston, thinks the date of the father's attack was between the 20th and 22d of August.

It is not difficult to explain this belief of the return on a certain day or even at a certain hour, if we suppose the patient has a preconceived notion with regard to the particular day or hour; he would then be looking for it, and he would have in addition all the influence of this preconceived notion upon a nervous system remarkably susceptible to such influences. There are other diseases in which a mental emotion is well known to produce an attack — asthma is one of these.

[1] *Case 24.* — Jacob Horton, Esq., who lives at Newburyport, Mass., near the sea-coast, writes as follows, September 26, 1865: "The past year (1865) has been a remarkable one — very dry and very hot. All vegetation is three weeks earlier than usual, and my catarrh came on just three weeks earlier (the first of August), and had all the characteristics, but moderate in degree, of course. I have no appetite, and but little sound sleep."

[2] *Case 19.* — "My first attack, which was when I was ten years old, commenced about August 15th, about the time the pollen appeared on the male flower of the Indian corn (maize). It was aggravated when cutting the stalks of the maize in the first week in September."

during the third and fourth weeks of August. In one case the first of September is given, but inasmuch as the date of termination is " October," it seems probable that both periods are a good deal uncertain; it is therefore so marked in the table.

That the commencement should vary is analogous with what we observe in other diseases, even those with a very definite course.[1] Eruptive diseases, typhoid fever, or even small-pox and measles, manifest themselves in different individuals after different intervals of time from exposure. We shall be still more inclined to this opinion when we consider the various causes which are known to be the excitants of single paroxysms.

§ 16. The periods of attack have been examined with reference to geographic or rather climatic relations; but the evidence is not sufficient either in exactness or in amount to draw any reliable inferences. Case 75, Mrs. S. B., and Case 4, Mr. T. H. Farnham, live near Philadelphia. The vegetation generally is two or three weeks

---

[1] *Case* 10. Author. — The dates of the attacks in my own case, are for several years in Cambridge, Mass., as follows: —

1842. August 19.
1843. August 20.
1844. August 18.
1845. August 16.
1846. August 16.
1847. August 18.
1853. August 14, itching in nose and ears; 21st, fully formed.
1856. August 19.
1858. August 21.
1863. August 20.
1865. August 13 slight; 20th, fully formed.

in advance of Boston,[1] and the difference of mean temperature of the two places for the months of June, July, and August about 7°.[2] The time of attack for Case 75

[1] *Time of flowering of the Peach, Cherry, and Apple, in Maryland, Pennsylvania, and Massachusetts, for three years* (" *U. S. Agricultural Report* "):—

1840.

	PEACH.	CHERRY.	APPLE.
Baltimore, Md.	April 5.	April 5.	April 24.
Paradise, Lancaster Co., Pa. .	April 16.	April 12.	April 22.
Cambridge, Mass.	April 25.	April 25.	May 4.

1842.

	PEACH.	CHERRY.	APPLE.
Baltimore, Md.	March 20.	March 25.	April 1–10.
Newtown, Pa.	March 27.	–	–
Cambridge, Mass.	April 23.	April 22.	May 8.

1844.

	PEACH.	CHERRY.	APPLE.
Baltimore, Md.	April 16.	April 12.	April 15.
Philadelphia, Pa.	April 8.	April 11.	April 14.
Cambridge, Mass.	April 27–30.	April 27–30.	May 4–12.

[2] *The Mean Temperature in Worcester, Mass., and Philadelphia, Pa., in June, July, and August, for 1865 and 1866. Worcester is about 2° 30' north of Philadelphia.*

1865.

	JUNE.	JULY.	AUGUST.
Philadelphia	77.3	78.3	75.9
Worcester	70.5	70.5	69.4

is stated to be August 19th or 20th,[1] and for Case 4 about
23d or 24th,[2] — the same date as that of the majority
of sufferers in Massachusetts. It may be, however, that
the plants, the flowering of which is best known, may not
have the same flowering time as those upon which the disease may depend; it would be unsafe, therefore, on these
grounds alone, to infer that it has no relation to vegetation.

§ 17. The manner of the first attack varies. With
some it is as severe as any subsequent one, and as sudden
in its onset.[3] In other cases the attacks are gradually
developed for several successive years, increasing regularly
in the severity of a single group of symptoms or several
groups.[4]

1866.

	JUNE.	JULY.	AUGUST.
Philadelphia	73.7	80.7	72.6
Worcester	66.	73.7	65.

[1] *Case* 75. — "My catarrh comes upon me annually in the night, between the 19th and 20th of August."

[2] *Case* 4. — "I have for the past eight or ten years spent my summer in
Beverly, about sixteen miles above Philadelphia, on the opposite side of the
river, going to the city daily. I have had catarrh since I was four years
old. It commences about the 23d or 24th of August, sometimes perhaps a
day or two sooner."

[3] *Case* 10. Author. — "My first attack was in 1833, the year I was
graduated at Harvard College; my second attack was when acting as an
engineer in the construction of the eastern portion of the Boston and
Albany Railroad. These two attacks were complete in all their stages, and
as severe as the subsequent ones. The disease seems to have come upon
me in all its force."

[4] *Case* 23. E. S. Dixwell, Esq., of Cambridge. — In 1848-50, I
discover by examination of my diary only that each year I complained in
August and September of weak eyes, in 1849 it was accompanied by herpes
zoster, and carbuncles. In 1853, my next entry, I was on a journey to
Niagara Falls, in August, from 5th to 15th, and suffered from catarrh in
part produced by irritation of the dust and cinders on the road. Afterwards
I was in New York City, and took one sixth grain of morphine for catarrh
without marked effect. In 1854 I was at the ocean side in July and Au-

The head first suffers, and not unfrequently the inference of the sufferer is that he is having an unusual cold in the head at an unusual time ; and it is not until the disease has increased in severity after a few successive returns, that he is aware of what has befallen him. Indeed, in some instances it gradually develops asthma in a severe form, and the patient applies for medical advice without the least knowledge of the true nature of the malady. The exacerbation in the railway train is so constant, that the disease is usually attributed to an ordinary cold taken in the train by an open window, increased by the dust and smoke, or to some other equally accidental cause.

§ 18. The disease may be divided into three stages. Some think they notice four stages — the first being a stage of incubation or development. But this is so rare and slight that it cannot be said to be proved.[1] It would

gust, returning to Cambridge August 12th, and experienced catarrh there slightly. In 1857 my diary speaks of "Hay Cold" as a recognized matter of experience. I was feeling very badly. Visited Gloucester at the ocean side with my brother, who was suffering as well as I. We were spoken to by the conductor of the railway train in sympathy because he had it too, and discussed the oddness of the disease and its prostrating effects.

This case, with the two following, illustrate the gradual manner in which it sometimes makes its first attacks.

Case 51. — "At the age of about twenty-five I began to observe that I caught cold, as I supposed, more easily in the latter part of summer and early autumn than at any other season of the year. This continued till about ten years ago without any marked change in my symptoms, and in the mean time I had resided in Central New York, New York City, and southern Ohio. On removing to Worcester County, Mass., my symptoms became more aggravated from year to year, and asthma, inflammation of the eyes, and what resembled influenza in its form, were added. Not till about seven years ago (after suffering about twenty-five years) did I learn what my real trouble was, or what to do for it."

Case 26. Joseph Peabody, Esq., of Salem, Mass. — Was first attacked in 1865, the last week in August, after a railway journey. The trouble was then supposed to be caused by the dust and smoke of the train.

[1] See note 1, page 25, for a description of a development stage.

Case 3. John J. Dixwell, Esq. — "The affection of the eyes in one year preceded by three weeks the more decided symptoms of catarrh, the eyelids becoming glutinous and uncomfortable."

be difficult to demonstrate it except by the accumulation of a considerable number of cases, because of the variations in the time of appearances of the disease, and of the approach of the separate stages.

The three stages may with propriety be termed *catarrhal, bronchial,* and *spasmodic.*

The first, the catarrhal, affects the eyes, nose, ears, and throat, producing the profuse watery discharge.

The second, the bronchial, affects the air tubes, producing cough, with more or less expectoration.

The third, the spasmodic stage, exhibits itself in the violent spasmodic cough, or the asthma, also most frequently spasmodic.

It is not to be understood that of these stages the groups of symptoms of each disappear before the succeeding stage comes on. They frequently run one into another, one or more stages overlapping. But the commencement of each stage is sufficiently distinct, even if it is added to those which precede, to attract the attention of the sufferer. Although all these stages are not necessarily gone through in each case, it must be admitted, after an examination of the table, page 33, that there is quite as great a uniformity in this respect as is usually found in disease. That there may be something real in these stages, depending upon a regular succession of annual influences during the critical period, seems probable. See note 3, p. 74.

§ 19. *Catarrhal Stage.* The approach of this stage is sufficiently distinct to warn the experienced sufferer of what is before him.[1] When it has once appeared, the consequences are certain for the whole period. Those who

---

[1] Rev. H. W. Beecher. " The attack often in the beginning comes on so suddenly that whereas at tea I am entirely well, in ten minutes after I am deluged with tears and flowings at the nose. In other seasons the inception is more gradual."

Daniel Webster. " The enemy may come as a thief in the night, or he may be as bold as a lion." — *Correspondence,* vol. ii. p. 463.

have had successive attacks prepare themselves for the storm.[1] They take refuge in places of safety, or arrange their affairs for the coming annoyances and disability.

The symptoms of this group vary in severity and in length ; they not unfrequently extend throughout the whole disease, but in a diminished form.[2] Generally the profuse discharge from the nose and eyes diminishes as the next stage appears, and becomes thicker and less irritating to the skin of the nose and to the upper lip. The itching gradually lessens ; but the inflamation of the eyelids comes on, if at all, towards the end of the stage, or sometimes later, when small abscesses occasionally form in them.

The febrile paroxysms and the headache do not usually appear at first — nor till this stage is fully formed.[3] They are most decided in the afternoon, or in the evening. At this time inability to work, mentally or physically, and the general feeling of being " used up " is most marked.

The nasal symptoms have their daily exacerbations depending upon the hour, or some internal causes.[4] They are most severe in the morning on first arising, or before the first meal, materially interfering with its enjoyment and sometimes actually preventing it by the difficulty of swal-

---

[1] Daniel Webster. "*Franklin, N. H., August* 10, 1851. I came to these regions on the morning of Thursday the 7th, thinking that the mountain air might strengthen me against the time when I expect my enemy, the catarrh, to attack me."

[2] *Case* 1. — " The discharge from the nostrils continues up to the very end of the attack, which is at the beginning of cold or coldish weather, say the first slight frost ; but the discharge is most severe about the middle of the disease."

[3] *Case* 20. W. H. Y. Hackett, Esq. — " This year (1866) I was attacked August 23d. It begins with sneezing, itching of the eyes and running at the nose. In a few days I have the symptoms of fever, a high pulse, hot palms, and sense of pressure upon the lungs. For a month I am unfit for business. I am a lawyer, and have on several occasions had to give over the trial of a case after it was opened."

[4] *Case* 73. Mrs. F. A. B. — " Paroxysms of catarrh begin about 4 P. M. I get a little sleep before 1 A. M., when I have a hard paroxysm which lasts sometimes two hours, sleep again and have another about 4 A. M., not usually so hard."

lowing. Besides this, there are certain external injurious influences. If there is dust or smoke, they are sure to prove a source of trouble. If the victim gives way to the great desire to blow his nose, and clear it of what seems to be an obstruction, he has probably prepared himself for a half-hour or an hour of discomfort. Once blow the nose, and the blood is forced into the tissues, they are distended, and the obstruction is worse than ever. It is important, therefore, to avoid this, and allow the limpid fluid to flow out upon a handkerchief; the vessels are then quickly relieved, and the fit is sooner over.

The eyes also have their exacerbations. While the nostrils suffer most in the early morning, the eyes are most in trouble in the middle of the day, when the light is brightest; they are better on a cloudy day, or during an easterly wind. So soon as the eyes begin to be suffused, the irritation finds its way to the nose, and the two begin to suffer in concert. The reverse action is seldom seen.

The irritation of the throat and of the ears seem to have exciting causes of their own. They are most annoying, on the whole, soon after an attack of sneezing; then the desire for relief by rubbing the palate with the tongue, or by attempting to swallow, is almost irresistible.

This stage continues normally eight or ten days before the second stage is entered upon.[1] It continues often

---

[1] *Case* 26th. Joseph Peabody, Esq., Salem, Mass. — "In 1866 I was attacked August 26th with itching and watering of the eyes, inflammation and swelling of the lids, especially of the lower lids; difficulty of swallowing continued two weeks, and was followed with cough and asthmatic breathing which compelled me to sit up at night. The obstruction of the nostrils obliged me to breathe through the mouth, producing a hard, dry tongue. These troubles gradually subsided and disappeared during the last week in September."

Case 4. — "The disease begins with great itching and irritation of the eyes and running thereat; then sneezing and running at the nose, which lasts ten or fifteen days, when it settles on the chest; the throat is filled with phlegm, breathing very laborious and difficult, with asthma for another fortnight, finishing with bronchial irritation which continues much longer."

beyond this, and even throughout the disease, diminishing in severity as time passes. But it does not diminish by regular steps; it has its time of sudden relief for a short period, and as sudden returns, raising hopes of a speedy recovery, that are not destined to be realized.

§ 20. *Bronchial Stage.* The bronchial stage begins about the end of the first week, or a little later; generally the first two or three days in September.[1] It is then that slight tickling or irritation at the top of the windpipe is felt, frequently accompanied by irritation of the throat, producing a slight hacking cough. This is felt only during the day, while the patient is moving about, and is more of an annoyance than a distress. It is without expectoration, or if any mucus is dislodged, it is in such small quantities that it is not thrown into the mouth. Though variable, it has no regular exacerbations. It would only be distinguished from a common cold on the chest by its irritative, tickling character.[2]

In a few days the cough becomes more constant and more annoying. The affection seems to have descended lower in the chest, and is attended with some pain. The first attempts at cough in the morning are now painful, with a tearing sensation beneath the breast-bone. Still, the expectoration is hardly to be noticed; it is transparent and without taste.

This stage is almost always accompanied with more or less of the symptoms of the first, and it is this combination which adds so much to the discomfort. The cough, how-

---

[1] *Case* 45. Dr. Anson Hooker's case. — " The cough and mucous expectoration does not come on till the attack has existed a fortnight or more."

[2] *Case* 16. — For twelve years has three weeks of irritation of the eyes, sneezing, inflammation of the mucous membrane of nostrils and throat, and then three weeks of bronchial cough with fever and copious night sweats, during which he has been greatly reduced in health and strength, so as to be confined to his bed, with a slight asthma, but not enough to prevent his lying down.

ever, is not increased by the other troubles, like the affections of the eye.

§ 21. *The Spasmodic Stage.* This first shows itself early in the third week, about the tenth of September.[1] The cough which up to this time had been frequent, but of an irregular character, begins to appear in paroxysms. These paroxysms may occur at any time in the day, but are much more certain to occur after the first sleep. On awaking with dry mouth and obstructed nostrils, after a little tickling of the throat, the paroxysm begins; the patient is obliged to sit up in his bed, or stand upright, and the attack frequently continues until, by the mechanical agitation of the stomach and nervous disturbance, retching is produced, and sometimes vomiting.

During the whole of this period the expectoration is scanty. A little glairy mucus or starch-like secretion is the only result of these violent efforts. Neither when obtained does it give the relief got by expectoration in an ordinary cold, or influenza. Obviously this is not the cause of the cough.

The nightly paroxysms of cough go on until the patient is wearied out, and the nervous irritability exhausted. Quiet then usually succeeds until morning, or until a fresh attack.

The muscles of the chest become sore from this violent action, and sometimes pain is felt in the intercostal spaces.

---

[1] Rev. H. W. Beecher. " The third stage is known by the tendency of the whole complaint to descend. It seeks to become bronchial. You are seized with spasmodic coughs. If you give way to them, they will leave you feeling as if a blunderbuss, loaded with shot, had been discharged through your lungs. A cough, like a breachy horse, should be ridden with snaffle (not snuffle) and curb, and never suffered to get under way, or to go faster than a walk. But it is not an unrelieved cough; for it alternates with asthma — a complaint in which a man feels, when asleep, as if some one was suffocating him with an unfair use of hemp; and when awake, as if the hemp grew inside of him, and he was trying with his breath to pull it up by the roots. Before you had busy days, but now you will have your chief occupation at night." — *New York Ledger,* September, 1868.

The spasmodic cough may be replaced, or accompanied by asthma.[1] Indeed, a slight wheezing, as though the bronchial tubes were slightly narrowed, not unfrequently accompanies the cough, even when there are no other signs of asthma, or with patients who never suffer from asthma throughout the whole course of the disease.

With some, from the beginning of the second stage, asthma is the most serious part of the disease, and in these cases it continues to the end. The attacks, like those of cough, are generally in the night on first lying down, or after the first sleep. If it has selected an hour for its invasion, it generally occurs at nearly the same hour during the remainder of the disease.

The attack is frequently preceded by a copious flow from the nose and eyes. At other times it comes on without flow of any kind, — a dry, difficult breathing, — compelling the sufferer to leave his bed for relief, or seek fresh air at the open window. In its character it does not differ from spasmodic asthma, coming on at other seasons of the year, or produced by other causes.

This also is the nervous stage, when there is irritability of the whole system, when little things annoy one, when sleep is disturbed, when the sufferer leaves his bed simply because he cannot stay in it.

As the last week in September [2] is approached all these

---

[1] *Case* 8. Daniel Webster. — "*September* 28, 1857, *Marshfield.* Sometimes the force of the catarrh seems pretty much broken, and then it returns, attacking the head, eyes, nose, etc., with great violence. I think it is approaching its last stage, which is the asthmatic stage. Some of our friends who are subjects of the complaint, and who have short necks, dread this."

[2] *Case* 8. Daniel Webster. — "*Marshfield, September* 20, 1848. I am so well to-day, and the weather is so fine, that if I get through the night without a paroxysm of catarrh, I mean to set the lark an example of early rising to-morrow, and listen to the ' murmurs of the Atlantic surge ' before the sun fairly purples the east." At other times it continued much longer. October 14, 1850, he says, " Tuesday, the 8th, I was to have gone into State Street to meet the people, but I did not find myself well enough.

symptoms are mitigated, and after a few days more disappear, not gradually and regularly, for that is not the character of the disease in any of its stages; but there are oscillations and intervals of rest from the annoyances, and these intervals become longer, and the attacks less severe, and so the whole disease vanishes. If, however, there is a succession of frosty nights, or one good black frost, the sufferer may, after a wretched early part of the night, awake in the morning entirely rid of his enemy.[1]

The next day (Wednesday) I came down to my home a good deal sick, and have hardly been out of doors from that day to this. My catarrh has held on unaccountably, and for three or four days last week I was quite ill with it, so much so that I called a physician."

Case 22. — "The attack diminishes with the approach of cool breezy weather, and generally gradually disappears during the latter part of September, but sometimes not till near the end of October."

[1] *Case* 57. Dr. Anson Hooker's case. — " The first good frost in October is a god-send to her ; she is at once relieved."

Case 68. — " The affection of the nose and eyes, and the asthma continue until about the first of October, or one or more heavy frosts ; the cough continues sometimes into November."

Mrs. S. D. P. — A sufferer from catarrh (case 72) states that her mother was also afflicted with the same disease until she was sixty-four. What was not a little remarkable, she was so sure that it ceased on the appearance of frost, that once finding herself suddenly relieved at two o'clock in the morning, immediately and confidently declared that there was a frost, which was true.

By an examination of the Meteorological and Chronological Register by Leonard Hill, a resident of East Bridgewater, Mass., it appears that for fifty-two years between 1806 and 1869, the average of the first frost noted was September 18th. The earliest frost in September was on the 8th, and the latest day without frost was October 3d.

The following dates for the first very noticeable early frosts in Framingham, Mass., twenty miles west of Boston, is from the *Boston Transcript*, 18 September, 1868 : —

1857	.	.	.	.	.	.	September 29.
1858	.	.	.	.	.	.	September 25.
1859	.	.	.	.	.	.	September 16.
1860	.	.	.	.	.	.	September 29.
1861	.	.	.	.	.	.	October 22.
1862	.	.	.	.	.	.	——— —.
1863	.	.	.	.	.	.	September 23.
1864	.	.	.	.	.	.	October 10.

The evidence of the influence of frost is pretty complete. Persons who have changed their places of residence to others, where the frost appears at a different time, find their day of relief also changed in accordance with it.[1] It is not to be inferred from this that relief does not occur until a frost, — it may occur earlier, —

1865	. . . . .	September 20, slight frost.
1866	· ·	September 24, hard frost.
1897	. . . . .	September 24.
1868	. . . . . .	September 18.

" The lines marking the limit of mean single occurrence of frosts closing vegetation are most difficult to place, and they can only be regarded as approximations. A temperature of 36° to 40° at sunrise is usually attended with frost destructive to vegetation, the position of the thermometer being usually such as to represent less than the actual refrigeration at the open surface. Taking the point of 40° as that which would give a frost in districts slightly more elevated and exposed than the posts themselves (where the observations were made), as the adjacent country usually is, and the comparisons for the month of September through the last twelve years [1843–1854] gives the following results."

" A line separating or detaching the coast of New England south of Boston, New York below West Point, the southern part of Pennsylvania, and extending through southern Ohio to St. Louis and Fort Leavenworth, would divide the districts of the Eastern United States, in which frosts might be expected in September, from those in which they would rarely or never occur in this month.

" The most southern points at which this measure of single extremes may occur, are at Baltimore, St. Louis, and Washington, and Forts Towson and Jessup, west of the Mississippi." See Lorin Blodget's *Climatology*, pp. 288, 289.

The line given above corresponds very well with that given by the cessation of Autumnal Catarrh. It is apparently not far from the southern line of the catarrhal region, as given on the map, which exhibits approximately our present knowledge of the extent of the disease.

[1] *Case* 43. G. H. H. — Born in Rockville, Maryland, thirty miles from Baltimore. Was first attacked when twenty-four years old, while living in Neretta, Ohio. Commenced August 28th. At first the whole disease ended in about four weeks; of late it has continued about eight weeks, beginning a little earlier, and lasting till October 20th, when frost occurs. Removed to St. Louis in 1864, since which time the attacks have been longer but less severe. Frost occurs in St. Louis later than in Neretta — about November 1st or a little earlier.

Case 65. — " The cold in the head and the cough cease, when I am in Philadelphia, with the first frost, about October 25th."

but the frost rarely fails to bring relief if it has not occurred before.[1]

The period of relief is thus stated in eighty cases : —

During the last week in September . .	19
By the first of October . . .	29
With the first frost	22
After first of October	10
	—
	80

The first frost occurs generally by the last week in September, the cessation of the disease in a large part of the cases is therefore nearly simultaneous with it.

[1] *Case* 69. — Miss E. W. thinks there is no connection in her case between the cessation of the symptoms and the appearance of frost. They sometimes cease before frost.

§ 22. NOTHING connected with this singular disease is more interesting than its relations to large tracts of territory or to places of less extent having a certain elevation above the sea level. In some of these places it can be shown conclusively that it exists, and in others, as conclusively, that it does not exist. In investigating these relations it is obvious that the number of facts should be large, while it is equally obvious that the small number, comparatively of persons liable to the disease, adds greatly to the difficulty of obtaining these facts; for none others than sufferers are competent witnesses, and these for only about one month in the year; none others are *catarrhoscopic*.

The evidence as to some places is sufficient, with regard to others we have the result of two or three cases only. The conclusions drawn from these cases, therefore, must be deemed probable only.

First, as to the occurrence of this disease in other countries than the United States. The " June Cold " was for a long time supposed to be confined to Great Britain; it is now said to exist in France, Holland, Belgium, Russia, Switzerland, and Italy, assuming that its identity is proved when it appears in these different countries at the same season, and with the same symptoms as in Great Britain. But in a disease in which, as we shall see further on, the predisposition of the individual plays such a prominent part, a stricter line of inquiry seems to be necessary; for this reason we have, as above stated, required the ex-

4

perience of the same person as to the influence of different
countries.

We have facts sufficient to show that persons suffering
from Autumnal Catarrh here do not suffer at the same season and in a similar manner in some other countries.

§ 23. *Great Britain.* The evidence is distinct with regard to several places in England. Subjects of the disease here, have been in Liverpool, in Manchester, and in
London, at the critical period, and have entirely escaped.[1]

In *Scotland*, at Balmoral and Stirling, and in various
parts of the Highlands and on the lakes, the travellers
saw no signs of their enemy.[2]

[1] *Case* 35. — Who had suffered from early youth till sixty-five years of
age, escaped the disease in England. He was much relieved at Long
Branch, although it reappeared on his return home after a two weeks' stay
at this sea-side resort.

Case 38. — Is twenty-one years old; has lived on the Hudson River, and
has had Autumnal Catarrh annually since five years old, except in August
and September, 1858, when in the vicinity of Manchester, England, in 1859,
in Aberdeenshire, near Balmoral, and in 1862, when in Halifax, Nova Scotia,
or on the water, between Halifax and New York.

Case 48. — "In 1866, left New York, July 21st, for England and Scotland.
I had no attack that year, nor the following year; but at the period it annually occurred a feeling of numbness about the head, giving the idea of sup-
pression, which disappeared with the appearance of frost. In 1869, again
in Europe, without evidence of Autumnal Catarrh."

Case 74. Miss A. C. B. — Was in the British Isles and in France
during the summer and early autumn of 1870. "I entirely escaped it for
the first time in my life. I went to Europe in April (the 22d I think), and
did not sail from there till October 6th, which, of course, was beyond its date
of continuance. I spent all the time in the British Isles, except a fortnight
in Paris, but I was in the British Isles through its usual time."

[2] *Case* 8. Daniel Webster. — He was in Scotland in August and September, 1839. The weather was cold, damp, and often rainy. He was
present at Lord Eglintoun's "Tournament," where everything was spoiled
by the rain, and yet he had no "cold" of any kind, — the only season he
escaped it from its commencement in 1832 to the year of his death, twenty
years after.

Author. — I was with my son in the Highlands of Scotland in 1869,
during August and September, and although it was very dry and dusty, we
neither of us experienced any inconvenience.

Case 4. — "I was never free from it for a whole season, until 1856,
when I was in the Highlands of Scotland."

France. This country has also been a place of safety. There is no evidence of a catarrhal affection at the critical period either in Paris or in the country.[1]

Switzerland is free from catarrhal influences — in the Tyrol, at Dole, and Geneva, and the country between.[2]

Germany was also visited with safety by persons suffering from the disease here.[3]

In most cases, the persons travelling in the countries just mentioned at the critical time of the year, were natives of the United States, but in one instance the traveller was

---

[1] *Case 74.*— After suffering from catarrh twenty-one years, in 1866 she went to Europe, and August 20th " was travelling from Berne to Paris. She sailed from Liverpool September 6th, and arrived in New York about the 16th. She was well during the whole period of her absence. Catarrh commenced on the day of arrival in New York, not gradually, but appeared in full force, as it would have been at that time had she remained at home."

Case 37. Frank B. Fay, Esq., of Chelsea, Mass.— "In 1858 I was in Europe. Left Paris about June 15th, travelled through Italy, Germany, and Switzerland, returning to Paris August 15th. I remained there three weeks, and went thence through England, Ireland, and Scotland, reaching my home in the United States, October 20th. During this year I had no Autumnal Catarrh. This is the only year I have escaped, although I think I have not had it as severely since. During the War of the Rebellion, I was in Virginia and Maryland, in August 1862 and 1864; I had it as usual."

[2] *Case 1.*— " In 1855 I was in Europe, and left Paris for Switzerland at about the period of the attack. After riding all day in the diligence from Dole to Geneva over a dry, dusty, limestone country, I arrived at Geneva in bad condition. All the next day I remained in my hotel taking laxative medicines, and on the following morning started for Chamouni. My troubles left me forthwith, and I had no more trouble that year."

Case 2. Rev. H. W. Beecher.— "The two summers that I visited Europe, I was entirely free from it. During the week that it was due in 1863, I was in the Tyrol. On the 17th of August it came, knocked, and looked in upon me, but did not stop. There was a single hour of mild but unmistakable symptoms, but only one."

Case 50. — Prof. Jeffries Wyman was on the Continent in 1870, without any evidence of the disease.

Case 23. E. S. Dixwell, Esq. — " In 1867 the period of usual attack of catarrh was spent in Switzerland without any appearance of the disease."

[3] *Case 12.* — Born in Germany, had suffered fifteen years in America, went to Europe, sailing August 5, 1860, and was in England, France, and Germany, but not on high land, for three months, including the entire period, and had no catarrh.

a native of Germany, who had suffered fifteen years in the United States and was quite free in his native land. He was again attacked on his return to the United States.

It may be assumed, therefore, with a good degree of certainty, that the Autumnal Catarrh of the northern portion of the United States does not exist in Great Britain, nor in those countries on the Continent above mentioned. To this we may add, that although Dr. Phœbus [1] makes mention of asthmatic and catarrhal attacks occuring in these countries annually, at other seasons than early summer, he makes no mention of a regularly recurring catarrh in September.

In *India* we have but one instance, that of a lady; she was well in Manilla or Batavia, but thinks she had a very slight trouble somewhat similar in Macao.[1]

§ 24. *United States.* We have already stated that the disease does not exist over the whole United States. It is a matter of difficulty to give the exact limits, the number of cases not being sufficient for that purpose. We can, however, arrive at proximate results which further observations may render more definite. We have no other evidence of its non-existence in certain places than this, that certain persons who have suffered elsewhere have ceased to suffer on removing to them.

A point which leads to misconception is the possibility and perhaps probability, that places on or near the limit may be so far influenced by the particular season as to be thrown one side or the other of the dividing line.

We must remember, also, that the determination of these lines may vary according as we select for our *catarrhoscope* one already suffering when he passes them, or one who has passed them before the critical period. It may require a longer time and different conditions to arrest a disease al-

---

[1] *Frühsommer-Katarrh*, p. 170.

[2] *Case 75.* — " Was also well in Manilla or Batavia, but thinks she had something resembling asthma without cough while in Macao."

ready in progress than are required for its prevention. Again, sensitiveness to the causes of catarrh may vary somewhat in the same person in different seasons ; this variation, however, is slight so far as our facts extend.

With these disturbing elements in mind, we proceed to give the probable limits of the catarrhal territory.

Beginning at the southeast, we may say that it extends along the Atlantic coast, which is everywhere low, from the Capes of Virginia in latitude 37° N., northeastward as far as Eastport, Maine, latitude 45°.[1] It cannot be traced into the white pine lands beyond the St. Croix River.[2] The evidence is sufficient to exclude it from New Brunswick, Nova Scotia,[3] and along the coast as far as Labrador,[4] beyond which we have no facts.

[1] Much evidence of the existence of the disease along the Atlantic coast has already been brought forward in the preceding sections. We shall have still more in the section which follows on the influence of the sea-side.

[2] *Case* 36. Henry G. Fay, Esq., Brookline, Mass. — "I left Boston, September 3, 1867, for Calais, Me., going by the way of Portland, Machias, and Eastport. My trip by rail was severe. I suffered terribly all the way to Portland. I went on board the steamer at night, and left the wharf at 11 P.M. for Machias. Although I had been so badly stuffed up in the nostrils all day, I slept comparatively well, and the next day, being still on the water, was comparatively well. I went to Eastport, Calais, and Houlton, Me. A smart frost occurred on two successive nights while I was in Calais in the middle of September, upon which the catarrh 'stepped out,' and I had no more trouble. I have found no relief at Centre Harbor, nor at North Conway."

[3] *Case* 44. James T. Hodge, Esq., Plymouth, Mass. — "In the summer of 1863 I was employed in Nova Scotia, and was a great deal upon the coast. On the 27th of August, the date of its annual return, at Cheticamp, on the coast of Cape Breton, I happened to be helping to get in some newly-cut hay to save it from a coming shower. No symptom of the asthma appeared then, nor did any appear until, on my return, six weeks afterwards, I began to sneeze in the cars on my way from Boston to Plymouth."

A New York gentleman who had suffered many years, escaped while in St. John, New Brunswick.

[4] A young man from Portsmouth, N. H., suffered while at the Isle of Shoals, and at Conway, N. H. For two years he entirely escaped on the coast of Labrador.

From the St. Croix, south of Houlton in Maine,[1] or about the line of six hundred feet elevation above the sea level, the line of exclusion turns eastward, following, approximately, the border of the elevation just mentioned, excluding the interior lakes of Maine, which are about one thousand feet above the sea, and descending towards the south, strikes the White Mountain region at its northern portion. Thence, turning towards the St. Lawrence River and running along the height of land which divides the waters falling into the Atlantic from those falling into the St. Lawrence, parallel to the St. Lawrence, strikes that river north of Lake Champlain. We have no reason to think the disease is found in Canada,[2] unless it be on the immediate northern shore of the lower Great Lakes, and between Lake Ontario and Lake Erie, but that the line of

---

[1] *Case 47.* — No relief at sea-shore; slight relief at Augusta, Maine; entire relief at Lake Umbagog, in 1860; at East Andover, twenty-five miles north from Lake Memphramagog, in 1862; at Littleton, near White Mountains, in 1866, in twenty-four hours after a hard ride in the cars; 1867–69, at Whitefield, at Mr. Dodge's, two miles towards Lancaster. "1870. I have been in camp in the eastern part of Maine and western part of New Brunswick, about fifty miles N. E. and N. W. of Calais, Maine, at the head of Passamaquoddy Bay, moving about from place to place, not in the vicinity of any settlement, and have been quite well. In 1863–65 I was in Cambridge, and suffered severely each year."

[2] Although we have evidence of its existence at St. Catharine's, on the western shore of Lake Erie, and at Port Hope, near Coburg, on the northern shore of Lake Ontario, and slightly at Murray Bay, on the St. Lawrence, the following cases indicate that it is not found generally in Canada.

Mr. P. informs me that a gentleman who had suffered six years, found relief in Montreal.

Case 40. — Left Glen House September 8th, after having been there a few days quite well, and went to Quebec, where he was also well.

Case 25. — Henry Rice, Esq., of Boston, was at Montreal, where he suffered slightly.

Mrs. R., whose case is recorded as No. 73, states that two other gentlemen from Boston were relieved at Montreal.

Case 41. — Was well at Montreal.

Case 11. — Mr. E. F. Atkins passed along the northern shore of the Great Lakes, on the Great Western Railway of Canada, during the critical period, without any evidence of catarrh, until he reached Albany, N. Y.

exclusion runs quite up to the southern border of the Great Lakes is clear, and along it to the south of the island of Mackinaw, between Lakes Huron and Michigan, in latitude 45° 51' N.[1]

It then crosses the lake and runs north of Lake Winnebago to St. Paul, Minnesota, at the junction of the St.

[1] *Case* 26. Joseph Peabody, Esq. — Was at Mackinaw, and was quite well at the Mission House, 120 feet above the Lake. He suffered as usual at St. Catherine's, four miles from Lake Erie, towards Niagara. Mr. Peabody informs me that a jurist from Chicago who suffered severely there, and also at St. Paul, Minnesota, got complete relief at the island of Mackinaw. Many others have been at Mackinaw with relief, even when it was active on arrival there. The island of Mackinaw is in the straits connecting Lakes Huron and Michigan. It is about nine miles in circumference, and rises on its eastern and southern shore in abrupt rocky cliffs, the highest point being about 250 feet above the lake. The fort is 150 feet above the lake, and 728 feet above the level of the ocean. There was formerly a missionary station here. It is now occupied as a hotel. It is upon a high bluff which faces the south. For the climate of St. Paul, see Blodget's *Climatology of the United States*, p. 73.

The following card confirms the above statement. I have satisfactory evidence that the disease here called " Hay Fever " is really Autumnal Catarrh.

" The undersigned, having themselves or in their families long been afflicted with that peculiar disease known as ' Hay Fever,' and having tried in vain the various prescriptions of many physicians, desire to testify for the benefit of sufferers from this disease, that we have entire immunity on this island of Mackinaw, Michigan. We find here many from different sections of the country of both sexes, and various ages, who have sought refuge from their annual August attack, and in not a single instance have they been afflicted here, — and some who have arrived here with the fever, were entirely free after a day or two. Knowing that there are numerous victims of this disease throughout the country, we think we discharge a simple duty when we thus make known a certain cure. The hotels here afford ample accommodations at reasonable rates, and the beauty of the island in its scenery, both of land and water, the delicious and invigorating air, together with its rambles in the woods, make it a delightful place of summer resort.

" GRANT GOODRICH, Chicago.
HENRY CHAMBERLAIN, Three Oaks, Mich.
HENRY W. KING, Chicago.
C. G. HAMMOND, Chicago.
" MACKINAW, Mich., *August* 29, 1871."

Croix with the Mississippi in latitude 45°,[1] leaving the Lake Superior copper regions beyond its influence.[2] From the Mississippi westward we have but little evidence, but what we have leads us to think it does not extend much beyond this great river, perhaps not beyond the alluvial deposit in its immense valley.[3]

[1] *Case* 9. Robert F. Fiske, Esq., St. Paul, Minn. — "Since I have been in St. Paul I have not known anything about an 'autumn cold,' such as I knew it at the East. At the East I suffered intensely from inflammation of the eyes, which inflammation extended all through that region of the head. I have not had anything of the kind here. At the East, usually for one full month, I was unfit for any duty, but now I am able to accomplish a full day's work every day, from the 1st of August to the 1st of October.

"In my judgment a person coming here merely to avoid having the cold at the usual time, would not wholly escape. I was East during the summer of 1859, and on my return reached home about the 20th of August, and brought back with me enough of the eastern influence to give me some trouble for two or three weeks."

[2] *Case* 74. — "I spent the last summer near Hancock Portage, Lake Michigan, in the copper region. My cold comes on usually August 20th, almost to a day. I had no sign of it while there. I left August 26th, went by steamer to Marquette, by railroad to Esconaba, by steamer to Green Bay, and by rail again to Chicago. Sunday, August 29th, I left Green Bay in the afternoon, and in two hours from that time I was completely in the clutches of the enemy. The cold was very severe, only a week or so, but after that it came on at irregular and unaccountable intervals till October 1st." She was then in St. Louis, Missouri.

Case 67. Mrs. D. — Was one year in the Lake Superior region, when the attack was shorter and much less severe than during the nine other years in Massachusetts.

Case 29. — Lived in Somerville, Mass., near Boston, and there suffered many years from unmistakable catarrh, from the last week in August to the last week in September. For several years in succession, during August and September, he was at Muscatine, Iowa, on the west bank of the Mississippi, at an elevation of 586 feet above the ocean. During these years he entirely escaped an attack, but on returning to his home, he was again attacked at the usual time, but less severely.

[3] *Case* 44. James T. Hodge, Esq., Plymouth, Mass. — "In 1870 I left Plymouth, September 5th, after having had the complaint about ten days, and was at Golden City, Colorado, at the base of the mountain, at about 6,300 feet elevation, on the 11th. I found no relief from it on the way to Colorado, and it continued apparently unabated for several days after I had been in the territory, at altitudes of 5,000 to 6,500 feet above the sea level.

Scale
English Miles

Explanation.

B.	indicates	Bay	B⁹ indicates	Burg
C.	"	Cape	P⁹ "	Port.
Gt.	"	Great	L. "	Lake.
Mt.	"	Mountain	N. "	New.
N⁰.	"	North	P⁹ "	Point.
St.	"	Saint	S⁹ "	Sound.
T.	"	Town	V. "	Ville.

in State Capitals
o Large Cities
o Cities and Towns
Political Boundaries

Green — General Surface of Land below 800 Feet Altit.
Brown — " " above 800 Feet Altit.

The western line may be traced southward as far as St. Louis, latitude 38° 37', near the junction of the Missouri

In the course of a week, however, it had very sensibly diminished, and soon disappeared. I was gone till the middle of October, and during my absence had occasion to travel over a good deal of mountainous country as far west as Utah, as high, I believe, as 10,000 feet above tide. I was entirely well, and have had no return of 'Hay Fever' since my return home, October 15th. I was surprised I should have had the complaint a week after reaching the mountains in Colorado.

"In the spring of 1865, I went to Montana, and for three successive seasons I escaped the disease. My wife was with me last year, and also escaped. We lived in a fine dry climate, at an altitude of 5,000 feet or more above the sea. The air was more delightful to breathe than I ever experienced elsewhere. My wife, who has had Autumnal Catarrh for sixteen years in succession, was in Montana in 1868, at an altitude of 5,000 feet above tide, and escaped it entirely."

Case 11. Mr. E. F. Atkins. — August 13th, 1869, he left Boston on a journey to Sacramento, intending to be absent from his home in Belmont, Mass., during the usual continuance of his catarrh. He went to New York well, riding in a railway "sleeping-car;" on awaking the following morning, perceived that he had a little cold in the head and throat, which ceased on reaching Pittsburg. The following morning, on awaking in the western part of Indiana, felt a slight catarrhal affection, which continued during his passage through Iowa, but on his arrival at Omaha (960 feet) on the 17th, he was quite well. He then passed over the uncultivated prairies of Nebraska to Cheyenne, in Wyoming Territory, on the railway, travelling night and day. On the 20th he took the coach from Cheyenne (5,800 feet) to Denver (5,200 feet), passing through Georgetown on the 21st. Ascended Grey's Peak (15,000 feet high) on the 23d, returned again to Idaho, which is about 8,000 feet, and on the 24th, by stage-coach, to Denver; on the following day returned to Cheyenne by a hot and dusty road, by which his eyes were irritated. On the 26th he again took the railway, and passed over the alkali plain, noted for its dust, with little annoyance. The next day he was on the stage-coach, on his way to Salt Lake City, which is 4,200 feet above the sea; here he stayed two days. On the 30th, left Salt Lake City in a stage-coach, for Unita, on the Pacific Railroad, and reached Sacramento on the 1st of September. After visiting Stockton, the Yo Semite Valley, and Nevada Falls, he returned to Sacramento, and set out for his return on the 16th of September, by the Pacific road. He was well till he reached the Mississippi River on the 22d, then unmistakable symptoms of Autumnal Catarrh appeared; instead of pursuing his journey directly east, he turned to the north, and reached Canada by the way of Chicago. On reaching Canada, and during his transit by railway through Canada, he was well. He arrived at Springfield, Mass., September 24th, and had

with the Mississippi, 1,253 miles from its mouth and 408 feet above the level of the Gulf of Mexico.[1]

The southern border probably extends from St. Louis

a sharp attack of catarrh, which ceased soon after reaching home on the following day.

This case is exceedingly interesting. We have here a line of observation extending across the continent from east to west, by a very sensitive *catarrhoscope*, making a complete section. We perceive that he was not affected after passing the Mississippi onward across the mountains to Sacramento, nor on his return until he again reached the Mississippi; then turning north, he passed by the catarrhal region to Canada, and travelling through that safe region, was not again exposed until he crossed the Great Lakes.

The following table gives the distances and elevations above the level of the sea, of some of the principal stations on the Union and Central Pacific Railroads, going east from San Francisco : —

Station.	Distance. Miles.	Elevation. Feet.
Sacramento	138	56
Colfax	192	3,448
Blue Canon	216	4,700
Cisco	230	5,911
Summit (Sierra Nevada)	243	7,042
Truckee	258	5,866
Reno	292	4,525
Wadsworth	327	4,104
White Plains	361	3,921
Winnemucca	462	4,355
Argenta	534	4,575
Carlin	583	4,930
Elko (Utah)	606	5,030
Pequod	689	6,180
Kelton	790	4,500
Promontory	828	4,943
Ogden	880	4,320
Unita	888	4,560
Rawlings	1,201	6,732
Sherman (highest point), Wyoming	–	8,100
Laramie	1,339	7,175
Cheyenne	1,396	7,040
North Platte	1,621	2,790
Omaha	1,912	965
Salt Lake City	–	4,200
Denver, Col.	–	5,200
Chicago, Ill.	–	600

[1] *Case* 74. Miss A. C. B. — Has been in St. Louis five years after suf-

eastward to Richmond, Virginia. We have evidence that
it does not exist at City Point on James River.[1] This
line may be extended still further eastward until it
strikes the Atlantic at the capes of Virginia. We have
also evidence that it does not exist still further south,
at Port Royal at the mouth of the Savannah River.[2] The
accompanying map of the United States is colored to show
the territory in which Autumnal Catarrh is found. The
uncolored portions are believed to be exempt.

Of these boundaries, the southern and western are the
least distinctly defined; they must be left as undetermined
until further evidence is obtained.

§ 25. As at present informed, we may assume that it is
a disease of temperate climates. It does not extend much
beyond the shores of the Great Lakes, certainly not into
the colder regions of Canada. Neither is it found in the
Southern States, that is, it is confined between the parallels
of 37° and 47° north latitude. But it does not occupy
the whole of this region ; it is not found in the extreme
east of the continent, nor does it extend to the far west.

§ 26. Its relation to the line of the southern limit of
early frost is interesting. According to Lorin Blodget,[3]
the lines marking the limits of mean single occurrence of
frosts during vegetation are most difficult to place. A
temperature of 36° to 40° at sunrise is usually attended
with frost destructive of vegetation, the position of the
thermometer being usually such as to indicate less than the
actual cooling at the open surface. There is great uniformity in the position of a line along which the thermom-

fering from Autumnal Catarrh in Massachusetts since eight years old.
She reached St. Louis about the last of August, and the disease continued
till about the first of October, being severe only the first week.

[1] *Case* 42. E. P. — Was well at City Point, Virginia, on James River.

[2] *Case* 45. C. F. W. — Was two years at Port Royal, at the mouth of
the Savannah River, during the War of the Rebellion, and escaped entirely,
although he again suffered after returning to Brookline, in the vicinity of
Boston.

[3] *Climatology of the United States*, p. 288. See note, p. 47.

eter falls to 36°–40° in the month of September at least
once in successive years. A line separating or detaching
the coast of New England south of Boston, New York below West Point, the southern part of Pennsylvania, and
extending through southern Ohio to St. Louis and Fort
Leavenworth, would divide the districts of the eastern
United States in which frosts might be expected in September from those in which they would rarely or never
occur in that month. The most southern points at which
this measure of single extremes may occur, are at Baltimore, St. Louis, and Washington, and Forts Towson and
Jessup, west of the Mississippi. In October, the extremes
are such that in any considerable series of years no portion
of the continent north of the latitude of New Orleans
escapes severe frost.

We see that the isothermal line of 36°–40° in September compares pretty well with that which divides the region in which the disease ceases in September, from that
in which it ceases, so far as our observations extend, in the
first half of October.

SEA VOYAGE.

§ 27. We have no evidence that any similar catarrhal
affection, during the critical period, attacks those who are
sailing upon the open sea. But we have several cases of
persons suffering in the early stages, who have ceased to
suffer within forty-eight hours after losing sight of land.
We have also the cases of those who, having almost passed
the critical period at sea, have suffered soon after landing
— sometimes within twenty-four hours.[1]

The severity of the disease in most of these last cases
has been thought to have been materially diminished, but
it has not ceased earlier in the season than has been its

---

[1] *Case* 62. — One year sailed from Liverpool August 14th, the attack usually commencing the 15th; landed in New York in ten days perfectly well;
within twenty-four hours the disease appeared and went on as usual.

wont. In other instances it has appeared in full force and
so continued. In a few instances it has been asserted that
the attack corresponded with the stage at which the disease would have arrived had the sufferer remained at
home; presenting, therefore, the spasmodic cough or
asthma, with the nasal symptoms combined or not, as was
the habit of the disease at other times.[1]

We have then reason to believe that a voyage in the
open sea during the critical period will prevent an outbreak
of the disease, or arrest it if it has already appeared in
force.

SEA-SIDE.

§ 28. Sea-side residence appears to have some influence
upon the disease, but very much less than a voyage across
the Atlantic or a cruise many miles from land. Many have
made the experiment of living directly upon the sea-shore
during the critical period, where they can be sure of the
sea air, and although in exceptional cases and in exceptional years considerable relief has been obtained, it has

---

[1] *Case* 1. — " In 1864 I was in London during the period of the attack,
and entirely escaped, not perceiving the slightest symptom; but having
returned home to Boston on October 1st, I was slightly affected after that
time, but only in the nose."

Case 75. — Was at sea on the way to India in August and September,
without symptoms of catarrh.

Case 62. — " Was on a voyage from Liverpool to New York during usual
time of attack, but had no evidence of disease until after landing."

Case 74. — " Left Liverpool September 6, 1866, and landed at New York
about September 16th. She had no indication of catarrh till the day of landing. The attack usually commenced between 23d and 30th of August."

Case 28. Hon. Lemuel Shaw. — Left Liverpool September 20th, and
landed in Boston October 1st. The attack then commenced and continued
till October 15th. The attacks usually began August 20th to 22d, and
lasted about seven weeks.

Case 54. — " Was entirely relieved from Autumnal Catarrh during the
three critical periods when she was at sea, in the months of August and
September."

Case 4. — " I was in England in August, 1850; embarked late in that
month for New York, where I arrived September 9th. I was entirely free
until I landed, when the catarrh came on and lasted till late in the month."

not been deemed of sufficient importance to warrant its repetition. Nor do those whose permanent residence is at the sea-coast escape.

Some, who admit that they have derived a certain amount of benefit from this position, declare that it is the cool, bracing air that gives them comfort and strength to resist their enemy rather than its actual removal.[1] Still, in some instances, where the residence has been far inland and a journey has been made to a city on the sea-coast, relief has been gained. Here, however, it is to be observed, that there is a double change, and it is difficult to assign to each its true influence. In this case a subsequent permanent removal to the sea-coast of Maine was followed by a diminution in severity.[2]

The extent of sea-coast under observation is very considerable; it extends from the capes of the Delaware in latitude 38° 30′ to Eastport, Maine, in latitude 45°. This last is near the eastern limit of the disease; and beyond this the coasts of Nova Scotia and New Brunswick, both those that border on the Atlantic Ocean and those on the Bay of Fundy, are believed to be free.

Some of the points along the coast, like Provincetown[3]

---

[1] *Case 1.* — "The sea-side only benefits me by being cooler; the mountain air seems to afford me a remedy."

[2] *Case 22.* Samuel Batchelder, Esq. — "While in New Ipswich in the interior of New Hampshire, I went to Boston several times to consult physicians, but was so much relieved while there that I returned without consulting them. On going home the disease returned. When forty years of age, I went to Lowell, and resided there six years. The disease was more severe during the time. I attributed it to the greater amount of dust to which I was exposed while building mills. I was obliged to go frequently to the sea-coast which always gave more or less relief. Went to Saco (when forty-six years old) on the sea-coast, where I resided fifteen years; the disease, though quite as regular in its attacks, was much less severe there, and on the whole has pretty steadily diminished in severity to this time. Since then I have lived in Cambridge, and have had the disease annually. Riding in the railway train produces a decided aggravation of symptoms."

[3] *Case 11.* Mr. E. T. Atkins. — Attack of catarrh came on August

on the extremity of Cape Cod, are insular in their relations to the sea ; Cape May [1] also projects far into the sea,
and should have an insular climate.   Others are actual
islands, like Martha's Vineyard or Nantucket,[2] which lies
twenty-five miles from the main-land.   This island is
about twelve miles long and four or five wide.   The Isles
of Shoals,[3] a group of islands six or eight miles from the

16, 1866, while he was at Cape Cod ; by the 24th it had become severe ;
September 10th it was at its height, affecting his eyes severely. From
that time his eyes improved, and the disease did not afterwards return in
force, although the nasal catarrh did not entirely cease till late in October.

    Case 8.   Daniel Webster. — " Since August 17th " (at Marshfield on
the sea-coast) " I have been more or less under the influence of my mis-
erable catarrh ; some days I have felt quite discouraged."

   [1] *Case* 4. — " I was at Cape May, mouth of Delaware Bay, one season,
and found my catarrh aggravated."

   [2] *Case* 57. — " Has tried change of residence during the attacks. She
tried first Nantucket (an island twenty-five miles from the main-land) and
was more comfortable while in the town of Nantucket proper, but not very
decidedly relieved.   The air at Siasconset, the extreme point of the island,
was too bracing or irritating to the mucous membrane of the throat and
bronchi already inflamed.   How it might have been if she had gone there
before the attack came on, is a question.   She has also tried the Isles of
Shoals, where the attacks have been milder, but not enough so to counterbalance the discomforts of being from home."

   Case 74. — " I was at Nantucket one year with apparent delay of the
attack, but next year a residence at the same island gave me no relief."

   Case 73. — " I left Fall River, Mass., for Edgartown on Martha's
Vineyard (an island) by advice of my physician, who said it was ' Hay
Asthma,' and caused by particles of vegetable matter, but I was worse
than ever before.   One year I spent the month of September in the city
of New York, and had it very much lighter."

   [3] *Case* 1. — " Two years ago I was troubled very much in Boston ; I
went to the Isles of Shoals [latitude 43°, opposite the New Hampshire coast,
seven or eight miles from the main-land], where I arrived much worse from
the journey.   I do not think I derived any benefit from the air there ; certainly I suffered more from the difficulty of breathing than ever before."

   Case 41. — Got relief from asthma at Isles of Shoals one year, but the
next year no relief.   In 1868 was well at Dalton, N. H., near White
Mountains.

   Case 72. — In 1863 she was relieved at the Isles of Shoals ; three years
after she was again there, but the asthma was worse than usual.

   E. S. Dixwell, Esq. — " 1860, August 22d, I went by medical advice to
the Isles of Shoals.   August 26th and 27th, the ' Hay Cold ' was very bad,

main-land, has a climate that assimilates much with the open sea. Fire Island,[1] on the southern coast of Long Island and fully exposed to the Atlantic Ocean, has a similar climate. Mount Desert is also fully exposed to ocean air.[2]

In few of these places do we find instances of relief, and in none of them is the relief certain.[3]

and I returned on the 31st not improved. The malady continued until the middle of September."

[1] *Case* 33. — A clergyman has been at Fire Island, near New York, without relief, nor has he obtained relief at the Catskill Mountains. He arrived at Gorham, September 4, 1867, and for the first time for five years that he had suffered from the disease, was relieved in two or three days. The relief was complete.

The Fire Island Hotel is said to be a great resort of New Yorkers who are affected with *Ophthalmic Catarrh*. But whether this is the "June Cold," or some other disease, I have not been able to learn.

Case 35. — Relieved at Long Branch, on the coast, about thirty miles south of New York.

Case 18. — Is better in damp, cloudy weather. At the sea-side, with an easterly wind from the sea, is better ; with a westerly or land wind, gets no relief.

[2] Prof. Jeffries Wyman. — Has during the past four years suffered from Autumnal Catarrh. The last year he was in camp in the Glen, and quite free until he reached Portland, September 24th, on his return to Cambridge. One year, while at Mt. Desert, off the coast of Maine, he went, after the disease had appeared, to an island in the bay, and was two nights in tent ; the weather was very damp and foggy, but the disease disappeared. The same happened after a visit to Otter Creek in the fog.

[3] *Case* 25. Henry Rice, Esq. — Resided in Roxbury, about four miles from Boston, where he went daily for the transaction of business as a merchant. At one time had a house at Swampscot, at the ocean side, but the suffering was so great while in the railway train between that place and Boston, that he was obliged to abandon the ocean side, and return to the city for relief.

Case 60. — "During several seasons I was at Nahant, Swampscot, or Newport, all of them on the sea, without relief."

Case 15. Edward Wyman, Esq. — Has lived in Roxbury and at the sea side, at Nantasket, during several summers, but never perceived any material difference in the severity of the symptoms in the two places.

Case 77. — She has tried going into the country and to the sea-side, but has noticed no difference in the severity of the disease. This year, 1868, visited Gorham, where the relief has been decided.

Case 19. — " I get no relief at the sea-shore during the attack."

Even the agreeable and healthful pastime of boating, which gives to the mind pleasant occupation, to the body gentle exercise, and a free exposure to the invigorating influences of sea air, affords no protection.[1]

The experiment has been tried of leaving a place of safety during the catarrhal season, and going at once to the sea-coast, in the hope that, being already free from disease, the ocean air might be enjoyed without danger; but it did not prove successful.[2]

We are therefore forced to the conclusion that the sea air has but little beneficial influence on this disease.

The influence of sea air upon the June Cold or " Hay Fever" of England is very different. Dr. Phœbus says: " Moist air brings to many, probably to most, great relief. Many praise the sea air. It brings a quick and lasting amelioration during the whole attack, even without sea bathing, which is also useful. Dr. Bostock proved this in his own case. Many reside at the sea-shore, or cruise about in yachts during the critical period. The asthma is immediately relieved at the sea-coast; but if the wind blows from the land, even for a single hour, the disease immediately returns."

---

[1] *Case* 44. James T. Hodge, Esq. — " The symptoms at Frostburg, Md., were just like those at Plymouth, where in 1868 I resorted to my sail-boat, in the hopes of alleviating them by constant exposure to the salt water. But the weakness attendant on the disease soon made me disinclined to the effort. I found no benefit from salt-water bathing."

[2] *Case* 75. — " Was at the Glen House in 1864, with relief, after finding no relief at the Profile House and Crawford House. In 1866 was well at the Glen House. The first week in September she went to Saco, on the sea-coast of Maine; was attacked with catarrh, and obliged in two days to return to the Glen House. The attack usually ceases in Philadelphia, her place of residence, about October 25th, the commencement of early frost. She obtained no relief at Crescent, in the Alleghany Mountains."

Case 71. — One year, September 7th, was obliged to leave the Glen House and go home to Lynn, Mass., a watering-place on the sea-coast, on account of domestic affairs; when within ten miles of the sea-coast, near Portland, was attacked with catarrhal sneezing and watering of the eyes. In two days she returned to the Glen House, was immediately relieved, and so continued.

The same is true of the early summer catarrh, or Rose
Cold of the United States, which seems much to resemble
the " Hay Fever " of England, without, however, being
identical with it.   Many suffering from this disease here,
obtain relief at the sea-side, so long as the wind is from the
sea.   The different effects of the sea air upon the Rose
Cold and the Autumnal Catarrh, is an important point in
the differential diagnosis between the two diseases, as will
be shown presently.

CITY RESIDENCE.

§ 29. In some instances considerable relief has been obtained from a residence in a large city during the period
of catarrh.[1]   But it is seldom complete, even in as large a
city as New York.   We have instances of relief in Boston, but then it is incomplete, dependent upon the direction of the wind, either from the sea or easterly ; and a
ride into the country for an afternoon is sure to be followed
by an attack.[2]   Many have undoubtedly tried the experiment of a city residence, on the supposition that the cause
of disease is to be found in vegetation, of which certainly
there is much less in the city.   If many of these cases have
been successful, they have not come to my knowledge ; I
have known but one of complete relief.[3]   Of those who
have tried it and failed, I have known many.[4]

[1] *Case* 1. — " I am much better in the city than in the country. I keep in
the city as much as possible."

[2] I know a gentleman of the legal profession, who has been relieved of
much of the severity of the disease by remaining in Boston during the
critical period. Still the relief is not like that which he obtains at the White
Mountains.

[3] *Case* 56.   Mrs. II. — In 1864, she went from the country to Boston,
and lived in Beacon Street, near the water, from August 15th to October
1st, and escaped entirely, although she walked frequently in the Public Garden. She then returned to Waltham, in the country, and remained free
from the catarrh. This was after twenty-five attacks of Autumnal Catarrh.

[4] *Case* 3.   John J. Dixwell, Esq. — " My first attack was while living in
Boston, and I perceived no difference in severity whether I was in Boston
or in the country in its immediate vicinity. It gradually increased in

NEW ENGLAND STATES.

By A. Guyot.

MOUNTAINS.

§ 30. In a previous section, large tracts of country have been pointed out where the disease unmistakably exists. In these tracts there are certain places of greater or less extent, in which, so far as known, it does not originate ; and a resort to which, at the proper season, prevents it in those who have previously suffered.

These places are, as a general rule, at a higher elevation than eight hundred feet above the sea level. But it should by no means be inferred that all places of this, or a greater elevation, are free from the complaint, or that places of less elevation are exposed to it. We have already shown that portions of country on the level of the sea are free from it. There are evidently other circumstances besides elevation upon which, or upon a combination with which, this immunity depends.

The first person known by me to have been relieved by a visit to the mountains, was a lady from Lynn, Mass. (Case 67 of the Table). She had suffered severely, especially in the asthmatic stage. She accidentally noticed, in 1853, while travelling in the White Mountain region, that her catarrh, which for twelve years had commenced August 20th, had failed to make its appearance. The following year she visited the same region before the usual time of attack, with the hope of escaping it. She did escape it. During the remaining ten years of her life, until 1864, she was at the Franconia Notch, White Mountain Notch, or at the Glen House, — most of the time at the latter place. During this whole period she obtained complete relief. In 1860, Jacob Horton, Esq., of Newburyport, Mass., who had suffered so severely that he was obliged to keep his room during much of the attack, in

severity at each annual return, and I found myself more liable to catarrhal affections at other seasons of the year."

Case 40. — " I have been in the city of Philadelphia, sometimes during the whole season, and at various places in the country, without relief."

answer to my inquiries, replied, " The only relief for me is at the White Mountains."

These facts drew my attention to the probable value of mountain residence. Other instances of relief soon became known to me, and persons suffering from this malady were advised to repeat the mountain experiment. They did so, and were successful.

It was afterwards ascertained that of those who sought the mountains, most were relieved, but not all. On investigating the matter, with a greater number of facts, it appeared that all places in the White Mountain region are not equally safe.

According to the evidence we now have, the line of safety includes the Glen,[1] Gorham,[2] Randoph, Jeffer-

---

[1] *Case* 4. — " In 1864, August 22d, I went to the Glen House with the cold and found entire relief; went up Mt. Washington and walked down to Crawford's on the 24th, got wet through, and while my luggage was coming round, was obliged to dry myself in the sunshine, but without any bad effect. I stayed at Crawford House and Profile House till September 1st, entirely well. I then went to Andover, Mass., *via* Littleton. The catarrh came on very badly in the railway train, and I suffered severely all through the month."

Case 40. — Has obtained no relief by visiting the sea-side; is relieved at the White Mountains speedily, especially at the Glen, and can then go to the Profile House with impunity. In 1868, having been at the Glen two days and three nights, quite well, went to Quebec, without any return of the disease.

Case 25. Henry Rice, Esq. — In 1862 first attempted change of residence. The first week in September asthmatic symptoms followed nasal catarrh and the affection of the eyes as usual, but more severe. He left Boston September 7th, and spent the night at Portland, suffering severely; next day reached Gorham, N. H. Was much relieved, and remained at the Glen House, 1,630 feet above the sea, till September 24th, then went to Springfield by the way of the Profile House. On reaching Springfield in the Connecticut River Valley was again attacked with catarrhal symptoms and asthma. Then went to Lebanon Springs, and returned to Boston well. 1863–64. Has been at the Glen House several successive years, making excursions up Mt. Washington and in the vicinity, and has had no trouble from catarrh on his return to Boston about September 27th.

[2] *Case* 26. Joseph Peabody, Esq. — In 1867 attack commenced August 23d and 24th. Suffered severely in railway train on the way to Gorham, where he had a severe night from obstructed nostrils and difficult breath-

son Hill,[1] Whitefield, Bethlehem Village, the Franconia

ing until 4 A. M., then much relieved. The ascent of Mt. Washington, August 30th, gave complete relief, which continued during the season.

Case 31. — A paper manufacturer, has had Autumnal Catarrh for twenty-five years. A niece also suffers from the same. Both are relieved by a visit to Gorham, N. H., and the vicinity of the White Mountains.

Case 64. — After having the autumn catarrh with severe asthma for six successive years, arrived at Gorham, August 14th, and remained till October 1st, without any asthma, and hardly a trace of disease.

Case 65. Mrs. M. — Arrived in Gorham the morning of September 15th, after a week's suffering from cough, and with the eyes much irritated; the following night was much better, coughed less, and in the morning awoke with eyes also improved, but with some discharge from the nostrils. The thermometer stood at 32°, a black frost, and Jefferson and Adams white with snow. In a day or two she was quite well.

[1] *Case* 3. John J. Dixwell, Esq. — " Each year since 1863 I have visited one or more of the various places of summer resort in the White Mountains, Gorham, the Glen House at the foot of Mt. Washington, the Crawford House, and the Waumbec in Jefferson, and during these three years I have had no attack of catarrh. I have had some slight irritation, not enough to annoy me, no irritation of the eyes nor throat, no cough. I arrive at the mountains from August 22d to August 24th."

1869. After being at Mt. Mansfield a few days, " I then went on to Jefferson ; suffered again in the railway train, and had another bad night at Littleton, though not so bad as before. I reached Jefferson on the 3d, and remained there till September 25th. For several days after my arrival had occasional attacks of catarrh, and my eyes were considerably inflamed, and through the whole month I had more of it than ever before at the mountains. Still my condition was vastly better than it had ever been in Boston during the same period, and, comparatively, I might call it relief."

A gentleman of Boston, with his wife, who had both suffered severely from annual catarrh, were at the Waumbec House in September, 1868. He was perfectly well for the first time in twelve years during the same period, and his wife (with the exception of a single day after unusual exposure), for the first time in twenty-four years.

Case 23. E. S. Dixwell, Esq. — " My attention being fully aroused, I find more minutes, especially as you had advised mountain air. *August* 14*th.* I feel the catarrh coming. 15*th.* Eyes and nose somewhat affected; dullness in the head. Off to Gorham, N. H. 16*th.* At Gorham, *no catarrh.* Continued quite well while at Gorham, except a slight rheumatism under scapula till September 1st. *September* 2*d.* Returned to Cambridge. *September* 4*th.* Have catarrh to-day ; 5*th,* badly ; and so it continued till the 20th or 25th. 1864. Went to Gorham, August 9th ; some inconvenience felt in the cars from smoke and cinders. The woods had been on fire for weeks previous. After I was in Gorham I felt nothing of catarrh. On September 1st, I removed to Jefferson Hill, Waumbec House, and stayed there till

Notch,[1] the White Mountain Notch,[2] and the various mountains within this line. Some have been relieved at Shelburne, and also at Bethel,[3] on the Androscoggin, but they must be considered as on the extreme border of the exempted region. Franconia Notch [4] is on the extreme

the 10th of September, when I returned to Cambridge. I was perfectly well all that time. September 15th, I note that I have catarrh, and on the 21st, I have catarrh badly. I thus give you, Doctor, all the facts I have recorded about my case. They indicate very positively that my case is remedied by the air on that side of the White Hills lying to the north."

[1] *Case* 1. — "In 1859 I went to the White Mountains, intending to be there when the trouble began, and to remain there some time. I escaped with merely the slightest symptoms of cold in the head, and was perfectly well for several days after the ordinary period of attack. Business, however, compelled me to return to town earlier than I had anticipated. I left the Profile House early in the morning perfectly well, and was perfectly well when I entered the railway train at Plymouth, N. H. But after riding an hour, my trouble commenced, and it had its regular course that year, accompanied by difficult breathing."

[2] *Case* 3. — In 1863, after trying the air of Gorham, went to Conway, and was taken badly with the malady, and sent by his medical adviser off to the north again. Went to Crawford's, and was relieved again.

Case 4. — "In 1865 I arrived at Crawford House, August 19th [he was then free from catarrh], and during my whole sojourn there till the 25th of September, I did not experience the first symptom of the approach of my annual cold."

[3] *Case* 58. — Mrs. B., of Belmont, Mass., was a week or more at Bethel, quite well, though she had a touch of the catarrh before leaving Belmont. Miss H. W. was well at Bethel, in 1871, but a visit of a day, six miles south of Bethel, brought on the catarrh; it was again relieved after her return to Bethel.

[4] *Case* 24. — "Last year (1864) I concluded to try the mountain air again. The fever came on very suddenly and severely, and I started in the cars from Boston the last week in August, for Franconia; when I arrived at Franconia, I was completely used up. A hard cough came on, and for nearly three weeks, I could neither eat nor sleep. It was a mistake going there; it is too low and damp; there were but two or three pleasant days from September 1st to the middle of October. I found the air in Boston more favorable, and soon began to mend, although I think there had been no hard frost. In 1854 I visited the Franconia Notch, and found it very unfavorable. I had a very hard cough for two weeks, and did not sleep more than two hours in the twenty-four, and with loss of appetite; of course very weak. I remained in Franconia till frost came; then began to improve."

Henry Rice, Esq., gives me the case of a lady who in 1865 went to the

southwestern border, and cannot therefore be relied upon in all cases.   Neither can immunity be claimed for Little-ton, Dalton, and Lancaster,[1] certainly not for those por-tions lying on the Connecticut and Ammonoosuc rivers. To the north and east, among the lakes of Maine, we enter the country already described as free from the disease.

Besides the White Mountain region, our knowledge of which is more complete than that of most other regions, there are other elevated tracts which are also safe.   Among these are Mount Mansfield,[2] in Vermont, one of the Green Mountains, and probably Stow Village, near its foot, although its elevation is said not to exceed seven hun-dred feet.   So also the Adirondac Mountains,[3] in the north-eastern part of the State of New York, including the St.

Franconia Notch without relief from catarrhal symptoms from which she had suffered several years, and returned to Boston.

Case 75. — In 1864 I was at the Glen ; my catarrh and asthma ceased during the first week in September.   I then went to Crawford's and the Profile.House, staying three days at each, but found no relief.

Case 62. — After being at the Glen House, has been also relieved at the Profile House ; another lady has also been relieved there.   She got no relief at the Catskill Mountains.

[1] Littleton and Lancaster I have myself tried but found no relief.   My stay, however, in the first named town, was short.

[2] *Case* 3.   John J. Dixwell, Esq. — *September* 25, 1868.   "Last year I left (Boston) on the 24th of August, for Burlington, Vt., going through in a day and wearing a veil.   It had rained the day before between Boston and Portland, but at Burlington they were parched up by a long drought.   I got the "cold" about twenty miles from Boston, had it all day, and had a dreadful night at Burlington.   It lingered about me there, and on the way to Stow, for two days.   On the 27th I went to the top of Mount Mans-field, and found myself entirely relieved, came down to Stow the next day, and remained there well for two days.   I found there a gentleman from Philadelphia, a naval officer, who had suffered from an annual cold for fifteen years, and was then nine days over his time without any cold."

[3] *Case* 49. — Has been at the Profile House without relief (1870).   Entered the Adirondac Mountain region August 15th, by the way of the valley of Boreas River (about 1,700 feet above tide), twenty miles from any culti-vated land.   Was perfectly well when he left the valley, September 1st. At Bullard's he met the first cultivated ground where corn was growing, about twenty miles from Lake Champlain.   In an hour he had the usual symptoms of catarrh.   After his return home, had more cough than usual, and was sicker generally, but the disease ceased September 25th, which is earlier than usual.

Lawrence and Chateaugay ranges, and probably the great
Pennsylvania and Ohio plateau,[1] which extends through
the counties of Madison, Cortland, and Tompkins, and
finds its greatest height in Chemung, Steuben, Alleghany,
Cattaraugus, and Chautauqua counties, are probably free
from the disease.   In these last it has a mean elevation of
about 2,000 feet above tide water; its valleys are about
1,500 feet.   The Catskill Mountain House,[2] 2,212 feet,

[1] E. S. Dixwell, Esq., during the four seasons he has been at Peterboro',
Madison County, N. Y., on the great Pennsylvania and New York plateau,
1,200 feet above sea level, has been free from any decided symptoms of
catarrh, and only occasionally slight intimations of it.   Once when he
drove down to Chittenango Falls, ten miles distant, and about 600 feet
lower, he returned the following day with unmistakable signs of catarrh,
inflamed eyes, nasal discharge nose-blowing, and hot skin.   These soon
ceased after a walk on the hills.

This plateau, over two hundred miles in length, is believed by American
geologists to have been the southern border of a great inland sea.   The
topography of the United States shows an immense basin, bounded on the
north by the range of mountains extending through Canada to the far West;
on the east by the New England range, extending southwesterly by the
Highlands of New York and the Alleghanies of Pennsylvania, thence west
and south towards the Mississippi River, and probably to the base of the
Rocky Mountains.   These presented a barrier to the inclosed waters of
1,000 to 1,200 feet above the level of the ocean.   The outlet of this sea, of
which the Great Lakes and the interior lakes of New York are all that
remain, was by the way of the Connecticut Valley; the Connecticut River
then equaling in magnitude the Mississippi, St. Lawrence, and Susque-
hanna, united.   See James Hall's paper in the *New York Geological
Reports*, 1840, p. 433.

[2] *Case 3.* Rev. Henry Ward Beecher. — " I have abundant evidence
that change, not of place, but of climate, will prevent it.   The Catskill
Mountain House is filled every season with fugitives from 'Hay Fever,'
and they find immunity — some of my friends escape it — by going to the
Adirondacs, and some by a tour through the Lake Superior region.
Fire Island Hotel is a great resort for New Yorkers who are affected with
ophthalmic catarrh.   Fire Island is about fifty miles from New York, on
the ocean coast of Long Island."

It may be a question whether a distinction is made here between the
"June Cold" and the "Autumnal Catarrh."

Case 38. — No relief at the Catskill Mountains, near which he resides,
nor at the sea-coast.

Case 48. — When residing in Brooklyn, N. Y., a visit to the Catskill
Mountain House gave relief.   After staying there three weeks, I returned to
Brooklyn, and again found my malady.   This occurred in two separate years.

affords relief to some.   Still further to the south, the Alleghany holds out places of refuge.   Although Frostburg, Md., in the Alleghanies, 1,050 feet, was ineffectual, a further elevation of 500 feet at Oakland, in the same mountains, answered the purpose.[1]

§ 31. Elevation is not the only element; this is shown by the fact that the high counties of Massachusetts do not give the relief that is got at the White Mountains, and on the elevated plateau of New York.   Stockbridge, among the Berkshire hills, at an elevation of about 1,400 feet, is no certain place of safety.[2]   The same may be said of the

Case 21. — "For about twenty years I was unable to find any relief except from change of climate, which was almost invariably obtained by a sojourn at the Catskill Mountains or in Western New York, during the period referred to."

The territory about the Catskill Mountains in which relief is found, is quite limited. A gentleman who was well on the mountain, was attacked immediately after a descent to Hudson River, about twelve miles distant.

[1] Case 44. James T. Hodge, Esq. — "Last summer (1870) I was at Frostburg, Md., 1,050 feet above the sea level. Suffered badly. A young man, native of the town, whom I employed as assistant surveyor, had it a second time there. He went to Oakland, on the Baltimore and Ohio Railroad, forty miles distant and 500 feet higher elevation (in a barren district), and found immediate relief. People from Cincinnati go there for the same trouble: one gentleman, an old sufferer from Cumberland, which is 600 feet above the sea level.

Case 75. — "On my return to Philadelphia I was again afflicted, and it continued through a part of October. We had no frost that year till November 12th. In 1867 I was at Crescent, among the Alleghany Mountains, one week in September. I had no relief; returned to Philadelphia, and was confined to my bed four weeks."

[2] Case 66. Miss C. C. — Had the disease with great severity in Stockbridge, Berkshire County, for eight years in succession. This town is about 1,400 feet above tide-water.

Case 23. E. S. Dixwell, Esq. — "In 1858 I had the disease at Lenox, Mass., August 20th; from that time till September 11th, it was very bad. In 1859 I had the Hay Cold in the Valley of Connecticut River."

"1861. Was at Sharon Springs from July 18th to August 21st. On the 17th I felt the catarrh coming on, and was advised to try smoking a cigar; tried it, and thought it did some good. But I did not follow it up much. After my return to Cambridge, the malady continued very bad, and I became much exhausted and weakened by it till somewhere about the third week in September. 1862, August 21st, I feel wretchedly with catarrh; stayed in Cambridge."

vicinity of Grand Monadnock,[1] near Lake Winnepiseogee, and the foot of Kearsarge Mountain, in New Hampshire. Mount Holyoke, 1,214 feet, on the Connecticut, in Massachusetts, has in one instance been beneficial.[2] To those interested in this question, the Table of Elevations of the main points in those regions will be found useful.

§ 32. The large number of persons, who have visited these regions successfully, demonstrate their safety. But we have other evidence : persons who have left them before the end of the critical period, have been at once attacked, and the attack has ceased immediately on their return.[3]

[1] In September, 1866, I went with my son to Grand Monadnock, in New Hampshire; ascended to the summit, 3,718 feet, and spent the night at the Mountain House, 1,600 feet, without relief to either of us.

Case 70. Miss H. W. — Was one season at the foot of Kearsarge Mountain, near Lake Winnepiseogee, without relief.

[2] *Case 57.* Dr. Anson Hooker's case. — "At Mount Holyoke she is pretty comfortable till the winds blow hard and the fogs come up on the mountain ; then she starts for home." Mrs. H. has since found relief at Gorham, N. H., near the White Mountains, at an elevation of 800 feet above the level of the sea, and this for several successive years.

[3] *Case 75.* Mrs. S. B. — In 1866 was at the Glen with relief; during the first week in September she went to Saco, on the sea-coast, and was at once attacked, and in two days obliged to return. She was again relieved. On the 25th of September she again went to Saco, after a frost there, without a return of catarrh.

Case 12. Mr. W. P. A. — A German gentleman, has been at the White Mountains always with relief; but if during the period of usual sufferings he goes to New York, he suffers while there and on the way there.

Case 69. — "I left Cambridge, September 2d, with unmistakable catarrh, and arrived at Dublin, N. H., at 4½ P. M., having suffered much in the train. 3d. Much relieved of the cold, but the irritation of the skin about the nose and mouth continued. 5th. Irritation much less, and at length entirely disappeared. 11th. I started for home perfectly free from any appearance of the catarrh, and continued so till I reached the outskirts of Fitchburg, when I began to sneeze, my eyes to smart, and the cold was again upon me in all its vigor."

Case 58. Mrs. J. B. — She suffers annually, commencing August 7th. In 1866 she was in Brunswick, Me.; well until August 16th. She then went to Bangor, Me., on the sea-coast, and remained well until September 5th, when she took the railway train for the White Mountains. She suffered severely on the road, and reached the Waumbec at Jefferson Hill the same

The change in a sufferer fully under the influence of his malady, on arriving at the mountains is sudden and striking. His first night's sleep is refreshing, and in the morning his most annoying symptoms — the itching and watering of the eyes, the sneezing and nose-blowing, or the asthma — have much diminished. A second night is usually followed by a day, in the course of which most of the symptoms disappear. If, however, the disease has continued until the mucous membrane of the nostrils and air tubes has become irritated and thickened, the disappearance of the effects of these changes is gradual. Besides this relief of the local symptom, a still greater change takes place in the spirits. Activity of mind and body replace discouragement and weakness, and the sufferer feels assured that he has at last shaken off his enemy.

The number of cases obtaining this relief in certain regions is too great to be explained by coincidence ; the repetition, year after year, of the same relief at the time of arrival in such regions, is conclusive that the relief is connected closely with the arrival; that the causes of the disease, whatever they may be, have ceased to be efficient. We have no evidence that persons, residents of these regions, suffer. We have also the still further evidence that

day. She was at once relieved, and remained at the Waumbec well until October 1st. She then returned to her residence at Belmont, in the vicinity of Boston, and was there a few days quite well. She then made a journey south, and on her arrival at Philadelphia was seized with the usual symptoms of catarrh. After remaining one week in Philadelphia and suffering severely, she went to New York, where she was again immediately well, and so remained. During her stay in Philadelphia, the flowers were in full bloom, and much like the middle of September near Boston.

It would seem, too, that there may be something real in the stages of the disease, depending, perhaps, upon a regular succession of annual influences acting at certain portions of the critical period, for some patients declare that if they leave the mountain previous to the usual termination of the disease they do not go through all the stages, but only those remaining incomplete at the time of return. How far this may be sustained by a considerable number of cases, I cannot say.

it is not dependent upon simple change of residence, in the fact that very many of those who are relieved have tried various other places without success; and yet these places, by their distance from their usual residence, and different physical conditions, should have afforded relief, provided ordinary change alone were required. They have also tried various kinds of drugs, and different methods of medical treatment, with as little success. An examination of the Table at the end of the volume will show the influence of residence in a considerable number of places, whether beneficial or otherwise.

We shall return to this subject in the section on treatment, where it more properly belongs.

There is another singular fact. Many of those who cannot eat fruit at home without a paroxysm, and those who cannot smell of certain flowers at home, can do both with impunity in non-catarrhal regions.[1]

We are forced to the conclusion, then, that the causes of a paroxysm of disease which exist elsewhere, are less active, or entirely wanting in the places above mentioned; and that those who visit these places in due season, are for the much larger part greatly relieved, or entirely free.

The line between the catarrhal and non-catarrhal regions is often quite sharply defined. A ride of five or six miles from Bethel to Albany, in the White Mountain region, was followed by an attack in the case of a lady, a subject of the disease, who was quite well at the former place. The same is true of the New York plateau and Catskill Mountains.

---

[1] *Case* 78. — "I cannot eat tomatoes nor peaches at home because of the soreness of the mouth and the swelling of the lips they produce; but at the White Mountains I can eat both tomatoes and peaches with impunity."

Case 63. — When at home in Lynn, Mass., the touching of a peach, pear, or melon, would bring on the head symptoms, sneezing, watering of the eyes, and irritation of the throat. During the last eleven years of her life the catarrh period was spent at the White Mountains, principally at the Glen House, where she was entirely relieved and could take fruit of all kinds freely.

The map of the White Mountain region opposite the title-page, illustrates the narrow limits within which safety may be found. The uncolored space represents those parts which, so far as we know, are exempt.

It is not to be inferred from what precedes that all cases of catarrh or asthma in autumn will be thus relieved. In the first place, there are other diseases which resemble that now in hand, which are not true Autumnal Catarrh, and are not cured by similar methods. And again, we can hardly expect, in the great variety of cases, both in severity and complications, that some will not prove intractable. And lastly, the physical character of these places may be temporarily so changed in temperature, moisture, or other conditions of the atmosphere, or vegetation, as to cease to be beneficial. That such should be the case, is in analogy with what we know of many questions frequently arising in medicine and physiology, in which nothing is absolute and invariable.

Nor should it be concluded that the places named above are the only places where relief is to be obtained. It is highly probable that many others will be found equally valuable, and perhaps in some of those pointed out the cure may be less complete than is now supposed.

§ 33. It is difficult to say upon what this disease depends. Many causes are assigned by different individuals, and sometimes several by the same individual. That these have an influence is very probable, but they are so numerous and varied that it is at once obvious that they are not the primary causes; that there is something more general underlying these, upon which they act as secondary or exciting causes.

Although we may not be able to arrive at definite conclusions upon this point, this should not prevent a careful investigation of the circumstances under which it appears, and so, perhaps, narrow the limits for a future and more careful study of a larger number of cases.

§ 34. *Sex.* Our table of cases shows us that the number of males greatly exceeds that of the females, fifty-four males to twenty-five females, more than two to one.[1] My inquiries have certainly had reference as much to the one sex as the other, and as they have been made in great measure at the mountains to which freedom from the occupations of the other sex would allow females more readily to resort, the probability is that the difference is greater than is here stated. Upon what this difference depends I am unable to say. If we suppose it due to the protection from atmospheric changes afforded by in-door occupations, we shall find further on that so far as males are concerned

---

[1] A similar difference in the liability of the two sexes is noticed in the June Cold of England and the Continent: of the 154 cases collected by Dr. Phœbus from various sources, 104 were males and 50 females. — *Frühsommer-Katarrh*, p. 8; *Die Krankheit ist häufiger bei Männern als bei Frauen*, p. 89.

such occupation appears to be adverse. The severity of
the disease is quite as great in the one sex as the other ; it
is not probable, therefore, that a larger number of cases is
overlooked in the one than in the other. Still further, it
is not noticed that the peculiar functions of the sex have
any influence in the˝time of attack, its course, or duration.

§ 35. *Age.* The following table exhibits the cases arranged with reference to age : —

Age when first attacked.	Males.	Females.	Total.
Under 10	11	0	11
10–20	11	4	15
20–30	12	13	25
30–40	4	4	8
40–50	8	3	11
Above 50	1	1	2

These numbers are too small to draw more than the
single general inference, that the disease belongs rather to
the early and middle periods of life ; of seventy-one cases,
fifty-nine commenced before forty ; of the remainder, only
two are known to have commenced after fifty. Females
appear to be attacked later than males.

With some persons the disease has diminished in severity as age advanced; with others it has gradually increased.[1]   I have never known any one who, having been
once attacked, entirely escaped a tendency to it, or who,
having been free while living, even for several years in
succession, in non-catarrhal regions, failed of an attack on
returning to a catarrhal region at the critical period.[2]

[1] The influence of age upon the severity of the disease, and also the relation of the disease to longevity, will be considered in the section on Prognosis.

[2] The June Cold, " Rose Cold " of England, is generally thought to
diminish in severity with age. In advanced life some of the symptoms
  ·irely disappear. This is most common with the throat symptoms ; al-
 ' ugh instances occur in which the eyes are quite well. Gordon says,
   [ay Asthma is never observed in the later periods of life." Bostock, on

§ 36. *Nationality.* Under this head we have but little information. All but two are American born, the others are Germans ; both were first attacked in this country, both escaped while on a visit to Europe during the critical period, and both after returning were again attacked at its next annual recurrence.

Only one instance of a colored person, a subject of the disease, has come to my knowledge.[1]

§ 37. *Profession or Occupation.* Here we have one of the many instances of the difficulty of arriving at accuracy in the matter of statistics, and this is a good illustration of their fallacy, unless other circumstances than the mere figures, arranged under arbitrary heads, are borne in mind. It is not always easy to determine the profession or occupation, inasmuch as it has not always been one and the same through life. In the following table, that is adopted as the profession which was the employment shortly before, and at the time of the outbreak of the disease. Several were occupied in the country, and out of doors, in early life, and sought the cities later, becoming merchants, or manufacturers, etc. ; so, also, of those who have become members of the learned professions, some were in youth pursuing the usual occupations of a country life. Both these classes would, under some views, and perhaps ordinarily, at the time of attack, be classed as farmers ; but as they had ceased to be farmers at the time of attack, the influence of that kind of life may be supposed to have ceased also, and they are classed according to the occupation then existing. It is true, we cannot say that change of occupation has no influence previous to attack, but we do know that it has little influence after it, for of those who have once been subjects

the other hand, says he never knew a person cured of it. Dr. Phœbus has no case which commenced after forty. *Typische Frühsommer-Katarrh,* pp. 74, 78.

[1] Mrs. B., herself a sufferer, and therefore well acquainted with the symptoms, reports to me the case of a colored child, the father an India Delaware County, Pennsylvania, who has Autumnal Catarrh and asth

of the disease, none have been known afterwards to escape it by such change, or by any other change than removal from the catarrhal region.

TABLE OF PROFESSIONS OR OCCUPATIONS.

Statesman	1
Jurist	1
Lawyers	3
Clergymen	3
Physicians	6
Professor of Anatomy	1
Dentist	1
School-teachers	3
Students	6
Banker	1
Bank Officers	2
Merchants	10
Manufacturers	10
Clerk	1
Gardener	1
Farmers	3
Carpenter	1
Butcher	1

It will at once be observed that by far the larger number above recorded have in-door occupations, requiring but little manual labor. Of the six who use their muscles most, three are farmers. It is not a little remarkable that of those who must make up the largest class in the community, so few should be reported as subjects. It may be that the disease with them is light, and therefore overlooked entirely, or not thought of sufficient importance to apply for medical aid. This, to a certain degree, is not improbable, for we find that physicians to whom application is made, do not all recognize it sufficiently, to ask whether the disease has recurred annually, nor do the patients think it

6

worth mentioning, even if it has been observed and remembered. It is by no means infrequent for a person to experience several pretty severe annual attacks before it occurs to him that probably they are returns of one and the same disease. Still, the mechanics and farmers of New England are too intelligent and too well educated to allow the disease to escape their observation entirely. If many applied for treatment at the *dispensaries* of the large cities, the fact would appear in their annual reports. No such disease is mentioned.[1]

I am inclined to think, therefore, that the disease is less severe or less frequent with those who labor, than with others whose employments are attended with less muscular exertion. The result, perhaps, of a life more in accordance with the rules of health, in this respect, for the mechanics and farmers of New England, as a general rule, are as well housed, clothed, and fed, so far as health is concerned, as those who are among the richer and in some respects more favored classes. This question, however, can only be satisfactorily settled when a knowledge of the disease becomes more general.

§ 38. *Family Predisposition.* It can be shown that some families suffer more than others from Autumnal Catarrh. It has also been observed that not unfrequently, while some members of a family have this disease, others have June Cold, or are subjects of spasmodic asthma at the same season or at other seasons, or to sudden and unusually severe attacks of difficult breathing, from exposure

---

[1] Of those affected with June Catarrh, or ".Hay Fever," Bostock says, " It is remarkable that all the cases are in the middle or upper classes of society; some indeed, of high rank. I have made inquiry at the various dispensaries in London and elsewhere, and I have not heard of a single unequivocal case occurring among the poor." George IV. of England was a sufferer.

Of the cases collected by Dr. Phœbus, it appears that a much larger number, proportionally, of those who were noble born (*Geburts-adel*), suffered than of the citizens, — 20 to 107. Of 154 cases, 146 were educated (*Gebildeten*), and only 8 uneducated.

to the fumes of sulphur in burning matches, the gases of burning anthracite, or the smell of certain medicinal substances like ipecacuanha; in other words, have a peculiar sensitiveness of the respiratory nervous system, a sensitiveness which points to a condition similar to that in Autumnal Catarrh, even if it do not actually develop it.[1]

In my own family, among the sufferers are my father, my two brothers, my sister, and myself; of three other children, only one arrived at maturity, a brother, who was exempt; my son is also a sufferer, and my daughter has June Cold.

Chief Justice Shaw was the only child of several who arrived at maturity; his mother had Autumnal Catarrh; of his four children, one son is a sufferer; a son and a daughter have June or summer cold. The son who has Autumnal Catarrh, has a daughter who is now twenty-two, and has had Autumnal Catarrh six or eight years. Another son who has arrived at maturity has neither summer nor Autumnal Catarrh.

Rev. Henry Ward Beecher has a sister, and his brother a son, who are sufferers.

The following are the family relations of sufferers: —

In one case, a sufferer had a great-uncle who was affected.

In one case, a maternal aunt.

In one case, both parents were affected.

In four cases, the mother.

In one case, one parent being a sufferer, three sons and a daughter and a grandson; one granddaughter with June Cold.

In one case, a daughter.

In one case, one son and a granddaughter; one son and one daughter with June Cold.

---

[1] I am at all times sensitive to the fumes of burning sulphur and to the smoke of anthracite. Both produce immediate and violent constriction of the air tubes, with wheezing, asthma, and, not unfrequently, hiccoughing, showing a decided influence upon the nervous system.

In two cases, each sufferer had a brother affected, the parents being free.

In one case, a sister and brother's son.

In one case, a brother's son.

In one case, a niece.

In a family in Plymouth, Massachusetts, three sisters, and in another, two sisters, are sufferers.

Of seventy-seven cases recorded in our Table, in fifteen (one fifth) more than one member of the same family is also affected, — a much larger proportion than exists in the community generally.

My inquiries may not have been as distinct upon this point, or the answers as well considered as they might have been; members of families who were young when reported may yet develop the disease. The probability, therefore, is that the family predisposition has been rather underrated than overrated. Further inquiries and larger numbers, here also, are needed.

As the facts now stand, it must be admitted that some families suffer more than others.

If this be so, it is not improbable that many of those who suffer are born with a predisposition; and it may be also that many others are born with a slighter or with the same predisposition, which, for want of sufficient exciting causes, fails to be developed. It may be, too, that the tendency remains dormant in one generation, to reappear in the next, in analogy with what is sometimes seen in asthma and some other diseases.

§ 39. *Individual Predisposition.* Having stated the general condition of those who are attacked, we see nothing in these conditions, either separately or taken together, which would warrant us in assigning them as the cause.

So, again, if we examine the other general influences that usually produce catarrh in those disposed to it, we find them acting upon numberless individuals without producing such marked, annually returning, and long continued

disturbance as we find in the comparatively small number
of persons who suffer from Autumnal Catarrh. Nor do
we know of any combination of these influences likely to
produce such a train of symptoms at such a time. Neither
do we find the individuals attacked particularly sensitive
to the physical agents that produce ordinary catarrh. On
the other hand, many of them declare themselves to be
healthy, and (as they believe) less liable to colds at other
seasons of the year than most persons.[1] They can expose
themselves with impunity even at the critical period, provided they are not in a catarrhal region, in a manner not
common with others.[2]

The disease is not essentially local in its effects upon the
system ; it cannot be controlled locally, and its very in-
tractability under such medical treatment as that to which
ordinary catarrh, in its first stages especially, not unfrequently yields, points to something deeper and more radi-
cal than can be supposed of a trouble merely local, — to

[1] *Case* 44. James T. Hodge, Esq. — "As to freedom from colds, I think
I have them much less frequently since these attacks. I very rarely have
one."

Case 1. H. W. Haynes, Esq. — "I never suffer from colds, or very
rarely, and enjoy good health, having never been sick, before an attack of
malarial fever caught this year on the bar of the Mississippi River."

Case 20. W. H. Y. Hackett, Esq. — "My general health is and always has been good."

[2] *Case* 4. T. H. T. — "In 1864 I went to the Glen House ill with the
'cold' (August 22), and found entire relief; went up Mount Washington
and walked down to Crawford's on the 24th, got wet through, and, while
my luggage was coming round, was obliged to dry myself in the sunshine,
but without any bad effect."

Case 10. Author. — My own general health I consider good, and think
myself less liable to ordinary colds than most people. My profession has
been a laborious one, and has called me to many exposures, both in summer
and in winter, by night and by day, with very little illness that could be
attributed to those exposures.

In 1868, 1870, and 1871, I have, with my brother, Prof. Wyman, and my
son, all of us subjects of this disease, spent the critical periods in tents in
the White Mountain Glen, upon the banks of the Peabody. We were all
not only without the Autumnal Catarrh, but without a cold of any kind,
and returned with better health and strength.

another element in the individual himself, — to *individual predisposition*.

§ 40. Let us now inquire as to the system or systems in which this predisposition may lie.

The mucous membrane of the eyes, nose, and throat is the seat of the first local outbreak ; but it is by no means certain that it is here that the disease really commences. On the other hand, there are certain sensations of a more or less definite character : weakness, accompanied by a sense of sinking at the stomach, palpitation of the heart, experienced by some,[1] which either precedes or closely accompanies the affection of the mucous membrane, indicating that the nervous system has already begun to suffer.

The suddenness with which the access commences, the violence and rapidity with which it invades different parts, the redness of the conjunctiva, the injection of its vessels, the profuse lachrymation, the itching, the irritation of the nostrils, copious secretion and stuffing, the irritative spasmodic cough, more like whooping-cough than bronchitis; the sudden spasmodic asthma, the itching of the skin, and the speedy disappearance of all these symptoms, without the usual signs of inflammation, certainly correspond better with what we know of derangements of the nervous system than with those of the mucous membrane, or the organs by which it is invested.[2]

[1] *Case* 41. J. W. D., Esq. — " The disease commences with a great sense of ' goneness at the stomach ' and palpitation of the heart. To these succeed itching of the nose, eyes, and throat."

[2] Any one acquainted with the investigations of Claude Bernard upon the vaso-motor nerves, will readily admit that a parallel might be run between the symptoms of Autumnal Catarrh and the effects of the experiments of this eminent physiologist on the great sympathetic.

Cutting, tying, or arrest of action of the great sympathetic is followed in a healthy animal almost immediately by increase of heat on the side of the head operated upon : the vessels are enlarged, congested, and beat with greater force ; the conjunctiva is red, the vessels injected, and the eyes tearful ; the nasal mucous membrane is also reddened, and under some circumstances pours forth a copious secretion ; the nostrils are obstructed, and there is a short cough. The glandular secretions, the local circulation,

There is no peculiarity of constitution, form, or condition of body observed in those predisposed. It attacks persons of all temperaments : those of light and those of dark complexion,[1] the light haired and the dark haired, those of large and those of small stature, the thin and the fleshy, the weak and the strong.[2] Neither is there any

and the sense of taste are disturbed, but not tactile sensibility. The changes of heat are sudden, follow at once, and are greatest immediately upon the application of the exciting cause. The vitality of the parts is exalted, and the action becomes like that of an organ passing into activity from a state of repose. In other words, the abolition or diminution of the influence of the sympathetic, instead of paralyzing, increases the energy of these acts.

According to Dupuy, in addition to these, there is infiltration of the limbs, and an itch-like eruption upon the skin, which ends in affecting the whole surface.

So, again, in experiments upon the fifth pair, the side of the face becomes red, the conjunctiva red and its vessels congested, although the temperature is lowered. Irritation of the superficial portion of the portio dura increases the secretion of the nasal mucous membrane and interferes with the movements of the soft palate. Claude Bernard, *Leçons sur la physiologie et la pathologie du système nerveux*, vol. ii. leçons xv.–xvi. 1858.

The integrity of the nervous system has long been held to modify growth and repair, and some dermatologists, availing themselves of the influence of the ganglionic system upon certain districts as regards nourishment and sensibility especially, consider the cause of herpes zoster (or *shingles*) an affection of this system, probably an irritation of the spinal ganglia or of the Gasserian ganglion. Isidor Neumann, *Lehrbuch der Haut-Krankheiten*, Wien, 1871, p. 147.

The eruption of herpes zoster generally follows the course of the nerves. Trousseau, *Clinique Medicale*, vol. i. p. 207.

[1] There are some remarkable peculiarities among animals in their relations to poisonous substances. Pigeons cannot be poisoned with opium, nor sheep with arsenic ; the bears of the White Mountains are known to eat tobacco freely and with apparent relish; the same is true of some kinds of mice.

But one of the most singular facts in this relation is reported by Prof. J. Wyman. The white hogs of Florida have a disease of the hoof, caused by eating the paint root, *Lachnanthes*, which kills it and makes it drop off. The *black* hogs, of the same breed, are not subjects of this disease. This is so well known that in buying swine contracts are made for black hogs only.

[2] The same want of characteristic mental or physical conditions has also been observed in those who are subjects of " Hay Fever " of England. Phœbus, *Typische Frühsommer-Katarrh*, p. 87.

Dr. Bostock says: " Those cases that have fallen under my own inspec-

peculiar mental condition, unless it should be thought that the Table of Professions indicates a tendency towards a higher degree of intellectual development. The only striking point is that it is more likely to attack those in good health than those who are ill.

Some patients have been impressed with the belief that this and some other acute sicknesses are incompatible, and cite instances in which they have themselves been ill of other affections at the critical period, and the Autumnal Catarrh has been arrested or delayed for the time being, to make its appearance subsequent to recovery.[1] In our search for a cause, then, we derive no assistance from condition of body or associated disease, and in this respect we are deprived of indications which are often valuable in the investigation of the causes of many other affections.

That the mucous membrane is implicated subsequently, is unquestionable. The great and rapid congestion of the erectile tissue beneath the nasal mucous membrane, not only explains the sudden obstruction and equally sudden relief of the nostrils under the influence of the vaso-motor nerves, but also shows how, under these repeated attacks, a congestive habit may be formed, and the tissue temporarily hypertrophied, or even permanently thickened.

tion have been generally of a spare habit and liable to stomach affections, but I have met with exceptions to this rule." "Hay Fever" — *Medico-Chirurgical Transactions*, vol. xiv.

[1] *Case* 66. Miss C. — "The third week in August I was attacked very severely with cholera morbus; for three days was severely ill; and did not entirely recover until the first of September, then the 'Hay Fever' came on; before the illness I had all the symptoms of the disease. I do believe 'Hay Fever' is a protection against other diseases. A person who had it a great many years, one year did not have it, and was very ill of typhoid fever and dysentery; the next year the 'Hay Fever' returned."

Case 45. C. F. W. — "One year had bowel complaint; the 'cold' did not appear until the bowels were well; it then came on as badly as ever."

Case 55. "One year, 1865, I was at Essex, on Lake Champlain, having a severe attack of Autumnal Catarrh; about 20th September I was seized with dysentery; the same day all catarrhal symptoms disappeared, and did not return that year."

The eyelids also become puffy, the edges of the lids dry and irritated, and the lachrymal glands are in an excited or excitable condition ; but these, like the mucous membrane, suffer later, and probably in consequence of the repeated attacks of congestion, as we have just stated with regard to that tissue.

We have already described the changes in the circulatory system, so far as the head is concerned. We have reason to believe these extend further than is obvious to sight. The heart certainly is in some individuals more easily disturbed by slight exertion during the period of disease, even when there is no reason to believe it is caused by any general loss of strength. In some instances, also, there are intermissions or irregularity of the heart's action, and a nervous quickness of beat, especially toward the end of the complaint. That these are not dependent upon organic changes is demonstrated by their cessation when the disease is avoided by change of residence.[1]

These expressions of disease, different from what we are accustomed to see in local affections, the absence of fever, the different degrees of severity in different individuals, and yet the conformity as to its time of commencement and duration, the little alleviation under any medical treatment, except that addressed to the nervous system, its sudden onset, its tumultuous course, and transitory character, lead us to suppose that the cause may act first upon the nervous system, and perhaps principally upon the great sympathetic.

§ 41. But, admitting that there is an individual predisposition, and that we have correctly intimated the system first attacked, we have made no advance as to the cause of the outbreak at a certain season of the year and at no other. We may say that the exciting cause or causes

---

[1] I was myself much annoyed, for several seasons, during the disease, by these intermissions, and a feeling as though the heart turned over ; I was also sensible of shortness of breath on ascending heights. These symptoms have disappeared since I have sought relief by change of residence.

do not exist. But here we are met with a difficulty. The causes which produce an access at the critical season, will not, as a general rule, even under favorable circumstances, produce a similar access at a non-critical season.[1] This we do not attempt to explain. We only know that it is in analogy with many other diseases. Affections of the bowels are especially rife in summer and early autumn, and accesses of disease are then produced by causes which at other seasons are harmless.

It has been thought that the cause of the return at a certain season is the summer heat. But the maximum of heat has already passed, and the nights have become cool, when the outbreak commences. The greatest heat, as a general rule, occurs in the last week of July, and, taken as a whole, that month is hotter than August. After the fifteenth, when by far the larger part begin to be ill, the heat has very materially declined, and continues to decline during the month of September, while the disease is worse, and so continues till frost appears.[2]

If it shall be said that the disease is the result of the preceding summer heat which has weakened the body, and so acted indirectly but efficiently, we can only answer that we have no evidence either for or against this view. It can only be said that whatever weakens the body at this season may open the way for other influences to become active. Those holding this opinion think the

---

[1] Dust and railway smoke, which are so very annoying to all sufferers, never produce the peculiar symptoms at any other season of the year.

Roman wormwood (*Ambrosia artemisiœfolia*), one of the surest excitants, does not affect me at other seasons, either in its dried or flowering condition. During the critical period it is almost unfailing. See note 2, p. 101.

[2] By the tables of temperature at Cambridge, Mass., for the months of July, August, and September, for twenty years (1820–1839 inclusive), we have the following means: July, 71°.9. August, 68°.6. September, 60°.3.

In 1869 (see *U. S. Agricultural Report* for 1869), the average temperature in New England was for July, 69°.1 ; August, 65°.6 ; September, 62°.2. The maximum of heat was about July 15th.

mountain air brings relief through its bracing and strengthening qualities, but the relief is sudden and complete, and before any considerable change in strength.

It has also been supposed that the relief at the mountains is due to the lower temperature of these more elevated regions. So far as the White Mountains are concerned, this supposition is not borne out by facts. The temperature of these regions is almost identical with that of the homes of some of those who obtain relief there.[1]

We can also show that if the disease were dependent upon the usual causes of catarrh, — changes of tempera-

[1] J. J. Dixwell, Esq., of Boston, to whom I am indebted for many observations, has given me the following record of the thermometer from August 20th to September 20th, made at the White Mountains, principally at the Waumbec elevation, 1,248 feet, and at Jamaica Plain, near Boston, elevation about 100 feet.

Mean Temperature at Jamaica Plain from August 20th to September 20th.

YEAR.	6.30 A. M.	3 P. M.	10. P M.
1856	57°.3	70°.6	60°.0
1857	75.7	70.7	60.3
1858	58.1	70.6	61.1
1859	53.3	68.0	56.3
1860	58.8	70.3	59.
Mean . . .	57.0	70.0	59.5

Mean Temperature at White Mountains from August 20th to September 20th, 1865.

YEAR.	6 A. M.	3 P. M.	10 P. M.
1865	54°.3	70°.8	59°.8

Mr. Dixwell remarks that the autumn of 1865 was considered uncommonly hot at the mountains.

ture, — the extremes of temperature at the mountains, so much greater than at the sea-shore during the same periods, ought, one would think, to develop it.[1]

So also of moisture. This is as great, probably, in many places which afford relief as in those which do not. Upon this point I have no observations, and can only express the opinion that those places where we have spent three seasons are no drier than our own residences.[2]

The stronger sunlight of the long days has been accused

---

[1] The following record was made in the White Mountain Glen, at about twelve hundred feet elevation. The corresponding observations at the Observatory of Harvard College were kindly given me by my friend, Prof. Joseph Winlock, the present eminent director.

AT WHITE MOUNTAIN GLEN.			AT HARVARD COLLEGE OBSERVATORY.			
1870. September.			1870. September.	7 A. M.	2 P. M.	9 P. M.
4	8 A. M. . .	68°	4	71°.3	84°.2	70.7
5	8 A. M. . .	58	5		74.1	61.7
6	8 A. M. . .	56	6	56.4	58.2	51.0
9	7 A. M. . .	29	7	52.7	72.4	56.9
	Sunset . .	76	8	50.0	63.2	53.6
10	7 A. M. . .	53	9	53.3	70.4	57.3
12		Water frozen.	10	58.6	65.8	
			11	48.7	64.0	50.0
13	Minimum	26	12	48.3	65.7	55.2
14	In sun .	112	13	45.2	73.6	59.7
15	Minimum .	34	14	53.5	76.1	60.8
	At noon . .	86	15	63.8	81.3	65.6
16	Minimum .	56	16	63.0	76.7	58.9
19	Minimum .	34	17	56.5	58.1	56.8
20	2 P. M. . .	74	18	59.0 ·	70.9	64.4
	4 P. M. . .	71	19		64.4	51.1
	Sunset . .	60	20	45.7	74.7	56.9
21	Minimum .	28	21	44.3	65.0	54.2
	Maximum, Sunset	77	22	52.3	76.0	59.5
22	Minimum .	32½	23	53.7	81.0	70.1
	Maximum .	78				
23	Minimum .	38				

[2] I here refer to the three seasons passed under canvas in the Glen on the banks of the Peabody River, with my son and Prof. J. Wyman.

of contributing to the production of the disease, even if
not of itself sufficient to produce it; and support has been
lent to both this supposition and that which attributes it to
the heat, because of the great annoyance from these causes
during the critical period.   But the days are as long, and
the heat we have seen to be no less, in regions which are
exempt than in others.

We are thus able to exclude certain influences from the
list of causes, by the simple process of exposing the patient
to these influences, in whole or in part, and finding that
the disease does not follow.

§ 42. There is one assigned cause which a very slight
consideration will show to be blameless, and yet it is from
its supposed connection with the disease of which we now
treat that it derives its popular name, — "Hay Fever."
Hay, in the temperate regions where the disease is most
generally found, is made in June or early in July; it has
therefore been carried a full month before the catarrh appears.   Further, in some elevated regions it is not made
until the arrival of those who seek relief, and yet no cases
have come to my knowledge of an attack arising from this
cause.   It may therefore be safely assumed that there is no
connection between it and the disease.   The term *Hay
Fever* is consequently inapplicable.

There are certain other supposed causes of which, on
account of their almost universal influence, we cannot so
easily dispose.   Dust and smoke upon the railway, or the
dust of cotton machinery or of the streets, some kinds of
plants, will be quite sure to precipitate an attack if near
the time of its usual appearance.[1]   So promptly does the
attack follow the exposure, that many persons assume with
great confidence one or several of these as the real cause

[1] *Case* 3. John J. Dixwell, Esq. — " The severity of the whole disease
varies somewhat in different seasons; the time of the commencement of the
attack depends somewhat upon accidental exciting causes : a ride in the
railway train with its smoke and dust, or a visit to a cotton mill, will hasten
the period of annual attack materially."

of the whole disease. But here, it is likely the predisposition has already existed, and these substances, as likely, act only as excitants, even when the disease thus prematurely brought on goes steadily through all its stages ; indeed, the fact that it will go through all its stages by whatever means excited, renders it probable that the real cause is already present. The experiment of residing in a large city has been made on the supposition, which I believe to be well founded, that catarrh is connected with vegetation, and it must be admitted that relief has, to a certain degree, been thus obtained, but it must not be overlooked that a large city differs from the country in many other respects besides vegetation which go to complicate the question. Still, it cannot be denied that there are probably those who, notwithstanding their predisposition, would have entirely escaped, were it not for some additional influence like that just mentioned. No one of the substances named above will initiate a similar train of symptoms at any other than the critical season.

No experiment, so far as we know, has yet been made in which the exclusion of a supposed cause has prevented the appearance of the disease at the critical period. If this can be done, we can then easily obtain positive evidence as to its origin.

It appears, then, that we know little of the origin of this singular disease. This is to be regretted. But we are to remember that even if we did know its origin and nature, it would by no means follow that our success in its prevention or treatment would exceed that we now have with our present knowledge of the character of its symptoms.

§ 43. THE exciting causes of paroxysms are much more easily and satisfactorily investigated than the real cause of the whole affection. These causes can be put in action at will, and the effect follows so promptly that there is less room for doubt. The experiments have, many of them, been repeated so often, and under so great a variety of circumstances, that little question can remain as to their connection with the subsequent phenomena. Many of these causes have already been mentioned among those erroneously supposed to be primary causes.

Among the most prominent and general causes of a paroxysm is the dust and smoke of a railway train.[1] This

[1] *Case* 21. — "Attack aggravated by railroad travelling, also by exposure to cool air after exercise, and by exposure to night air; diminution of strength, accompanied by great lassitude so long as the affection continues. My lungs, ears, and throat are not affected. It commences with sneezing, itching within the nostrils, watering of the eyes, and free expectoration, most severe night and morning."

Case 4. — "Dust, railway travelling, heat, and sunshine, increase the paroxysms in frequency and severity."

Case 22. — "Riding in the railway train produces a decided aggravation of symptoms. Much relieved by rainy or damp weather."

Case 63. — "Is annoyed by dust in sweeping a room, or the dust of the highway. New hay does not trouble her."

Case 72. — "I had dreaded to travel by rail fearing that the inevitable dust would bring on the trouble, though travelling by rail in Europe (at the same season) did not cause it at all. I was attacked on the boat.

"Was the disease in an incipient form in me, only waiting for an exciting cause which was found in the dust, or was it in the atmosphere between Green Bay and Chicago? I did not perceive any amount of dust."

Case 66. — "I am most comfortable when I have a piece of thick Swiss muslin, wet with water, tied over the nose and mouth. I most particularly avoid dust."

The fuel for locomotives on railways is wood or anthracite coal. The chemical constitution of the smoke must be different, but the effects seem to be the same.

trouble is so general that few fail to mention it as among the greatest of their annoyances. The dust of the highway on a windy day is another source of trouble, but less than that just mentioned. Whether it be that this last depends upon mechanical irritation alone, while the other, being a compound of chemical and mechanical irritants, acts in a double sense, we do not know, but with most sufferers it certainly takes precedence of all others. The dust from straw or hay is deleterious to some, and to others the dust from sweeping a room. These troubles are sometimes so great. as to require that the face shall be covered with wetted muslin and the nostrils filled with pieces of wetted sponge while exposed to these causes. Some speak of the slightest movement over the face, a slight draft of cooler air, or the passing of a hair over it, as bringing on an attack of as much severity as that from any other more general cause.

Strong light, sunshine, especially falling upon the face, will produce a violent paroxysm of sneezing, and the other symptoms follow in quick succession. Even the moving from shade to sunshine, when it is not otherwise annoying, will do the same. Opening the eyes in the morning especially, if accompanied with movement, is equally provocative of an attack. The influence of strong light upon those sensitive to it is more sudden in its action than any other. Where it does not produce a paroxysm, in the weakened state of the eyes, it produces so much pain that it must be avoided. In some instances the nervous apparatus of the eye is so sensitive that the sufferer confines himself for days to a darkened room.[1]

[1] *Case* 8. Daniel Webster. — "*September 8th*, 1851. Yesterday and Sunday were exceedingly hot, bright days; the heat affected my eyes much, after the catarrh fashion. I resisted the attack, however, by the application of ice.

"When the sun is very bright I am obliged to avoid going out on account of my eyes, except, indeed, when the sea is calm and I am protected by an awning. The bracing air of the ocean I find very beneficial."

Case 35. Henry G. Fay, Esq. — "In every case coming under my own observation I have found that the hot sun adds fuel to the fire."

So much relief do some get during dark and cloudy weather that they declare that the darkest days are their brightest.   This relief, however, should not be altogether attributed to the diminished light, for such days are more likely to be damp, if not rainy, and this diminishes or entirely stops another great enemy, the dust.   Hot, dry, dusty, and windy weather is on the whole most to be dreaded.[1]

This is not true of all; some are much worse during damp weather; it produces chilliness, hoarseness, and cough, and they are obliged to confine themselves to their houses and comfort themselves with artificial heat.[2]

Fruit of various kinds, pears, peaches, plums, melons, and the stalks and flowers of potatoes, are all charged by some individuals with producing paroxysms.   Some are liable to attacks after eating or smelling one kind of fruit, to others several kinds are injurious, but by far the greater

Case 77. — " Sunlight produces sneezing.   I sneeze most on first rising in the morning ; warm weather will increase the paroxysms."

Case 1. — " I keep in the shade.   The sunlight makes me sneeze."

[1] *Case* 1. — " The attacks are aggravated by hot, dry, and dusty weather, especially while riding in a railway train.   They are relieved during damp, rainy, or cold weather.   The hotter and drier the season, the greater are my sufferings."

Case 4. — " I am better during and after a cold rain-storm than in dry and dusty weather."

I have myself long noticed that I am better on a rainy day than on one that is bright.

Samuel Batchelder, Esq., in a note suggesting that the disease may depend upon the influence of the pollen of certain plants which flower at the critical period, says : " My own experience has been that damp, or even stormy weather, such as may be supposed to diminish the floating of such particles in the atmosphere, has uniformly afforded relief, even when the complaint was most severe."

[2] *Case* 45. Dr. Anson Hooker's case. — " She is better in quiet dry weather ; is worse in damp, windy, or dusty weather.   Heat or cold does disturb her."

Case 8.   Daniel Webster. — " In such a day as this, — a northeast rain-storm pouring, — I cough a little and am as hoarse as a frog.

" If the weather is wet or damp, I must stay in the house, and have a little fire to prevent fits of sneezing and nose-blowing."

7

part of the subjects of catarrh are annoyed by none of these things.[1]

Some are sensitive to the fragrance of flowers. While one suffers in " aromatic pain " from a rose, another can enjoy the rose, but finds an enemy in the geranium or the heliotrope. This sensitiveness is not the same throughout the year ; with most it is entirely wanting, except during the critical period, and as a general rule it is less in non-catarrhal regions than others.[2]

---

[1] *Case* 71. — When at home in Lynn, Mass., the touching of a peach, pear, or melon, will bring on the head symptoms : sneezing, watering of the eyes, irritation of the throat. The last eleven years of her life during the catarrhal period, from August 20th to October 10th, has been at the White Mountains, principally at the Glen House, where she was entirely relieved, and could take fruit of all kinds freely. She was also relieved at Crawford's and the Profile House.

Case 38. — Suffered severely in Morristown, New Jersey, when the peaches were ripe ; is always worse when in the presence of this fruit.

Case 75. — The smell of fruit — pears, apples, peaches, grapes — during August and September, will bring on an attack of asthma.

Case 11. Mr. E. F. Atkins. — Cannot eat fruit in autumn. Bartlett pears, which ripen early in September, produces, when eaten, itching of the throat, and impairs the voice. But these troubles are less when the fruit is eaten without the skin. When in California, September, 1869, could eat fruit freely, especially pears.

Case 78. — Cannot eat tomatoes nor peaches at home, because of the soreness of the mouth and swelling of the lips they produce. Can eat both peaches and tomatoes at the White Mountains with impunity.

[2] *Case* 57. Dr. Hooker's case. — " When eighteen years of age first noticed being affected by the aroma of roses. The following year while picking some roses, she felt an itching in her eyes — this was in the morning, — the itching increased, and in the afternoon was so intolerable that she asked medical advice. After this she could not be in a room where there were bouquets or many flowers, without itching of the eyes or other catarrhal symptoms. She has often been obliged to leave an omnibus when large bouquets were present. This state of things continued ten years before she began to have the regular Autumnal Catarrh. After this she was not so sensitive to the aroma of flowers, still she could not be much in their immediate atmosphere and not feel their influence. We can never have many flowers in the house unless covered with glass. I will add that all fruits in an uncooked state, except strawberries, inflame the mouth and throat, and bring on itching. If melons, tomatoes, etc., are sliced and placed upon the table, they must be removed. If she hands an apple or an orange, the eyes

Some persons who have been debarred from fruit for the greater part of their lives, have enjoyed it freely at the White Mountains during the catarrhal period.

The Indian corn (maize) when in flower produces sneezing and other evidence of a paroxysm with some individuals, and also after it is fully ripe. The cutting of the stalks, or being among them, will have the same effect.[1] If the Indian corn were a cause of the disease, as a whole, it would appear at different times corresponding with the appearance of the pollen. Indian corn is planted early for summer use, and ripens more than a month earlier than for

and nostrils are immediately in trouble, and this at any season of the year. She was subsequently at the White Mountains during the critical period, and was much less annoyed by these causes than when at home at any season of the year."

Case 1. — " I find that the scent of full-blown roses makes me sneeze, and once I was picking strawberries in a hay-field in July, and suddenly found myself attacked by a violent fit of sneezing and running of the eyes, but it soon left me after I had bathed my head in cold water, and retired to a cool room."

Case 58. — In 1866 she left the White Mountain region October 1st, quite well, for Belmont, Mass., remained a few days, and then went to Philadelphia. Immediately on her arrival she was seized with the usual symptoms of Autumnal Catarrh, which did not abate until she reached New York a week afterwards, when she entirely recovered. The flowers were in full bloom in Philadelphia during her stay there.

[1] *Case* 19. — "My attack commences about August 15th, about the time the pollen appears on the male flower of the maize. It is aggravated by cutting the stalks of the maize in the first week in September, when the cough begins. This is worse nights and mornings. I have asthmatic breathing in September, at times severe, compelling me to sit up during the night."

Case 69. J. B. F. T. — " I had spent a part of the sensitive period in the Adirondacs, in the valley of Boreas River, from the 14th till the 29th of August, without a symptom. In coming home, when within fifteen or twenty rods of the first ploughed field, about fifteen miles from our camp, I commenced to sneeze, and in less than an hour the cold was in full blast." It is true that the Atlantic district of New York is more fruitful of Indian corn, averaging $32\frac{1}{2}$ bushels to the acre, and here the Autumnal Catarrh flourishes. But the central and western district, including Madison County, yields 25 bushels to the acre, quite enough to have an influence upon the disease, if dependent upon it, and yet persons with the disease elsewhere, here escape it.

the usual farm crop. The disease does not appear sooner near the large cities, where this early crop is most abundant, than in the country. It is true this grain is not raised in any quantity in the mountains, but there are other places, on the great New York plateau, for instance, where it is cultivated in large quantities, and where this disease is not found. It cannot, therefore, be looked upon as more than a cause of paroxysms; indeed, the number of persons in whom it produces these effects is comparatively small.

Although the hay produces no ill effect, there are certain plants which flower later than the haying season, which are believed to have a very decided influence. The thistle, the golden rod, and especially the weed known as Roman wormwood, hog-weed, bitter-sweet (*Ambrosia artemisiæfolia*), are known to aggravate the disease and produce severe paroxysms.[1]

The very general impression that the Roman wormwood is a cause of the whole disease, has led me to experiment upon its effects. It flowers in the open air about the middle of August or a little later, and continues to flower till late in September; it is covered with a large quantity of a fine pollen which is constantly shed during the flowering season; an approach to it, during the critical period, will produce a paroxysm with a very large number of persons. This, with the fact that its flowering corresponds with the critical period, lends strength to the supposition that it may

---

[1] *Case* 66. — "I believe the thistle and golden rod (*Cirsium lanceolatum* and *Solidago*) affect me, and when the frost has blighted them I breathe more freely; after three or four frosts I am entirely well."

Case 18. — Roman wormwood produces irritation in the throat and asthmatic breathing; he cannot work where it is; he is irritated even by passing in the road near a field in which this weed is growing.

Case 15. Edward Wyman, Esq. — Has observed that the proximity of Roman wormwood will bring on an attack; the odor of peaches seem also to aggravate the trouble. Damp night-air is prejudicial.

This plant is the only one that I have ever known to cause an attack in my own case; and this will invariably bring it on from very slight exposure.

be a real cause. It grows very generally in those regions where the disease exists, and most luxuriantly near the sea-coast. It grows very sparingly in mountainous regions, and is then generally short and feeble.[1]

Most causes of paroxysms, like fruit and flowers, cease to produce their specific effects, with most persons, in non-catarrhal regions. With this plant it is not so, a majority of those exposed to it experience a paroxysm nearly as severe in the one region as the other.[2] These are the

---

[1] *Ambrosia artemisiœfolia* of Linnæus (Roman wormwood, hog-weed, bit-ter-sweet) is thus described by my friend, Dr. Gray, the distinguished Pro-fessor of Botany in Harvard University: "Much branched (one to three feet high), hairy or roughish pubescent; *leaves thin*, twice pinnatifid, smooth-ish above, paler or hoary beneath; fruit obovoid or globular, armed with about six short acute teeth or spines. Annual. Waste places everywhere, July to September. An extremely variable weed with finely cut leaves, em-bracing several nominal species." — *Manual of the Botany of the Northern United States*, by Asa Gray, Fisher Professor of Natural History in Har-vard University, Cambridge, U. S. New York, 1859, p. 1.

[2] Early in September, 1870, I gathered in my grounds at Cambridge, Mass., some Roman wormwood in full flower, covered with pollen, taking the whole plant, stalks and roots. This was carried to the White Mountain Glen, about 1,200 feet above tide, where we remained till September 23d in the afternoon. The parcel containing it was then opened and freely sniffed by myself and son. We were both seized with sneezing and itching of nose, eyes, and throat, with a limpid discharge. My nostrils were stuffed and my uvula swollen, without cough, but with the other usual symptoms of Autumnal Catarrh. These troubles continued through the night, and did not disappear till the afternoon following. Prof. Jeffries Wyman, who was of the same party, did not sniff the plant, and had none of the symptoms just described.

A portion of the same plant was sent to my friend, J. J. Dixwell, Esq., at the Waumbec House, Jefferson Hill, who has kindly sent me the follow-ing results: —

"Eight persons sniffed the plant. One was seized with asthma and stricture in the chest, and did not entirely recover from the effects until the next day. This person is severely affected with asthma, and particularly sensitive. One was attacked with catarrh, as he would have been at the same period at home, and the eyes were irritated for several hours; one had sneezing and coughing for some little time; two had sneezing only. One had sneezing and watering of the eyes; one had only irritation of the eyes for some time; one experienced no effects whatever; eight other per-sons were in the house at the time who are subjects of the disease, they did *not* sniff the plant, and were not similarly affected."

principal facts in support of the theory that it is a cause of the whole disease.

On the other hand. It has been planted in February, has flowered in July, a full month before the ordinary time of catarrh, kept in the sleeping-room of a subject of the disease while in flower without effect.[1] It has also been gathered with care when in full flower, preserved in its dried condition in a bottle, and sniffed late in February, also by a subject; it was followed, in one experiment, by some stuffing of the nostrils and discharge of a limpid fluid, but perhaps no more than might follow many other irritations of the nasal mucous membrane ; in another it had no effect.[2] It is very wide-spread, and is found from Canada to Georgia, and from Maine to the Rocky Mountains, covering many places where Autumnal Catarrh is not known to exist.[3] It is true the plant may have different properties in different regions, as is the case with Indian hemp and the common hemp of the United States, and also, to a certain extent, with tobacco. I am inclined to give weight to this view.[4] But still, with our present knowledge, Roman

Mr. Dixwell says, " I think I have been quite as much affected by pears, peaches, and apples in my room, as I was by the Roman wormwood."

[1] In February, 1865, I planted in a pot a quantity of the seed of the Roman wormwood (*Ambrosia artemisiæfolia*), and kept it in a warm room ; as soon as the weather was suitable it was placed out of doors and properly cared for. It began to bud early in July ; 16th July it was in flower ; the pollen was apparent but not copious. It was then placed in my sleeping-chamber, and there remained until it ceased to flower. Nothing which I could attribute to its influence followed.

[2] I made the experiment upon myself February 25, 1871. As it has not been repeated either upon myself or another, it must be taken with the reservation that should attach to all single experiments in physiology.

[3] Dr. Gray has kindly furnished me with the following places from which he has specimens in the Herbarium of Harvard University : Halifax, Nova Scotia ; Bridgewater, N. Y. ; the New York and Ohio plateau, 1,000 feet elevation, common ; Buffalo, N. Y.; Illinois; Saskatchewan River; Spokan River; Great Plain of the Columbia, Washington Territory ; Pennsylvania ; Blue Ridge ; Table Rock; South Carolina ; Cooper River; Texas ; Mexico ; Cuba. It is not found in England, France, or Germany.

[4] In September, 1871, at Woods' on Moore River, near Randolph Hill,

wormwood can be regarded as only a very active and general cause of paroxysms, but not a cause of the whole disease.

Attacks like those of Autumnal Catarrh may be produced undoubtedly by many other vegetables besides those above mentioned. One fell under my own observation, in which they followed immediately after the eating of a few chestnuts ; they had also occurred previously, after eating filberts and English walnuts, and after a meal of buckwheat cakes. The only nuts which can be eaten with safety are almonds and hickory nuts.[1]

§ 44. The poisonous influence of some vegetables is beyond doubt. The two varieties of *Rhus*, *Radicans* and *Toxicodendron*, are well known instances of violent and

---

I passed without disturbance a garden in which Roman wormwood was growing quite luxuriantly for the White Mountain region; my son had also been frequently at the same place at the same season, with impunity. I cannot but think it would have troubled us if it had the same properties as that raised in Cambridge, and sent to the Waumbec House at Jefferson.

[1] October 13, 1870, Mrs. R., light hair and light complexion, about thirty-five, ate two raw chestnuts and two or three boiled ones. In about five minutes, while walking home, had pricking in the mouth, throat, ears, and eyes, with lachrymation, also obstruction of the nostrils and a watery discharge. These symptoms increased, and in about five minutes more had a violent cough, with slight expectoration and sneezing. The throat was obstructed apparently by spasms, making it difficult for her to swallow. She had pain in the abdomen resembling colic. I saw her in half an hour from the beginning of the attack. She was then coughing violently, the nostrils were obstructed, the conjectiva red, the vessels injected, the velum red, and the uvula swollen, most near the velum. There was still pain in the abdomen, but less. These symptoms gradually subsided, and in an hour from the commencement, had nearly ceased.

She had a similar attack when four years old, after eating hazel-nuts ; this was repeated two years ago. Cannot eat filberts or English walnuts, or other nuts which have been in the same dish with them, without these symptoms. Almonds and hickory nuts are the only nuts she can eat with safety. Cakes of buckwheat, when eaten, produce violent sneezing, watery discharge from the nostrils, irritation, and redness of the eyes, and pricking of the throat. These symptoms begin within an hour after the meal, and continue two or three hours. This lady was not a subject of any form of annually recurring catarrh.

long continued affections of the skin, produced in some
persons by handling the plant, and in others by merely
passing near it, affections so closely resembling erysipelas
that they are only to be distinguished by the absence of
constitutional symptoms.

The question as to the probable origin of this disease,
whether in the vegetable or animal kingdom, inevitably
comes up and requires examination. The principal reasons for a belief in the vegetable origin are as follows: —

1. It has a fixed season for its appearance, when the
heats of summer have developed and ripened most of the
plants of the regions where it exists. The time of commencement does not vary more than the time of flowering
of many plants.

2. The fixed time of disappearance, which is when vegetation declines.

3. Its disappearance immediately upon the appearance
of frost. This is also strengthened by the fact that a person who is perfectly well in a non-catarrhal region, or in a
place where there has been a frost, will be at once attacked, during the critical period, if he visits a place which
has had no frost, and again as quickly relieved if he returns.[1]

[1] *Case* 75. Mrs. B. — She is relieved in Philadelphia as soon as frost
appears, about the 25th of October. In August, 1866, she was at the Glen
House completely relieved ; the first week in September she went to Saco,
and was so ill that she returned in two days, and was at once relieved, and
so remained. No frost had occurred in Saco. September 25th, she again
went to Saco and she was well ; a frost had occurred. She went to Philadelphia in October, and was again troubled ; there had been no frost there.
Her trouble continued until frost.

Dr. Hooker's case. — Her troubles last till the first good frost in October.
This is a godsend to her, and she is at once relieved. Compare the experience of Mrs. J. B., note 2, p. 99.

That some persons get relief before the appearance of frost, is certainly
true; but it is also generally true that vegetation has then begun to decline,
and it is not unreasonable to suppose that the cause or causes may already
have gone through their active stage. So far, then, this is an argument
in favor of vegetable origin.

4. The relief, to a certain extent, sometimes obtained in the middle of large cities, where there is little vegetation.

5. The existence of the disease in certain regions only.

6. Its entire absence at sea.

The last three arguments cannot be considered as of great weight, inasmuch as the conditions differ in many other respects besides the diminution or absence of certain vegetable influences.

§ 45. It cannot be proved that the disease may not be of animal origin, and the following may be considered as reasons in its favor : —

1. Insects may exist upon the plants which flourish most during the catarrhal period, and die or become dormant at the same time and under the same influences.

2. The eminent physicist, Helmholtz, states that for five years past he has found in his own nostrils during the June, or " Rose Cold," from which he suffers vibrios (infusoria usually classed with animals, but of doubtful origin), which are expelled after a violent sneeze, and exist at no other time. He has, he thinks, also proved that the disease may be prevented or arrested by a quinine solution, which destroys infusoria.[1]

---

[1] From *Virchow's Archives*, vol. xlvi., part 1, February, 1869, p. 101, for the use of which I am indebted to my friend, Dr. Calvin Ellis, I translate Helmholtz's letter. It is in the article on Quinine (*Pharmakolgische Studien über Chinin*), by C. Binz, Professor at Bonn. "I have suffered, as far as I can recollect, since 1847, from a peculiar catarrh, called by the English ' Hay Fever ; ' the peculiarity is in this : that it makes its attacks during the hay harvest (in my case between the 20th of May and the end of June), that it ceases in cooler weather, and, on the other hand, quickly becomes very intense if the sufferers expose themselves to heat and sunshine. Then comes an extraordinary sneezing and a copious irritating discharge with a throwing off of epithelium scales. This increases after a few hours to a painful inflammation of the mucous membrane and external nose ; fever arises, with headache and great lassitude, if the patient does not withdraw from the heat and sunshine. In a cool room the symptoms subside as quickly as they came, and for some days there remains but a slight discharge and sensitiveness owing to the loss of epithelium. I remark here that all other years I have very little tendency to colds or to catarrhs, while the ' Hay Fever ' has never failed for twenty-one years to attack me at the time of

3. Dr. Charlton Bastian experienced all the prominent symptoms of " Hay Fever," after dissecting a parasite of the horse.[1]

the year just mentioned, neither earlier nor later. The case is extremely troublesome, and increases to an extremely severe indisposition if the patient is obliged to expose himself much to the sun.

"The odd connection of the disease with the time of the year, led me to think organized beings might be the cause. On examining the secretions during the last five years I have found regularly certain vibrio-like bodies, which I have not observed in my nasal secretions at any other time. In the accompanying drawings I have figured the most common forms. They are very delicate and small, and can be seen only with the immersion lens of a very good Hartnack's microscope. The characteristic of the commonly isolated and single joint is that it contains four nuclei in a row, of which two are more closely united pairwise. The length of the joint is 0.004 mm.

---

[1] Dr. H. Charlton Bastian (*Philosophical Transactions*, vol. clvi., 1856, p. 583, note), describes the effects invariably produced upon himself whilst working at the anatomy of *Ascaris megalocephala* from the horse: "Emanations from this animal had the most decided and poisonous influence upon me, and this not only when the animal was in the fresh state, but after it had been preserved in methylated spirit for two years, and even then macerated in a solution of chloride of lime for several hours before it was submitted to examination. I first examined this species in the spring of 1863. The effects were a greatly increased secretion from the Schneiderian membrane with irritation of it, causing continuous sneezing, irritation of the conjunctiva, itching about the eyelids and caruncula lachrymalis; great desire to rub them. Rubbing immediately gave rise to a swollen and puffed condition of the eyelids, swelling of the caruncula, and extreme vascular injection of the conjunctiva; if the rubbing was persisted in, actual effusions of fluid would take place under the conjunctiva, raising it from the subjacent sclerotic and cornea (?) A few minutes would suffice to produce these serious effects upon the eyes, but after a little bathing with cold water and rest in a recumbent position for a couple of hours, they would again have resumed their natural condition. At the same time that these effects were produced upon the mucous membrane, the skin of the face and neck was also affected so as to cause a sensation of itching, something similar to what exists in a mild attack of nettle-rash." Subsequently he had a species of asthma. "My system became at length so sensitive to the emanation of this animal, that I was even unable to wear a coat which I had generally worn during these investigations, without continually sneezing and suffering from catarrhal symptoms. In two months the symptoms ceased, and did not return till the next May, when it continued six weeks into June. Dr. Schneider and other anatomists were not affected in this manner."

This attack strongly resembles the June Catarrh of England, and as it occurred at the usual catarrhal season, it might well be questioned whether it was not that disease instead of the effects of the parasite.

4. The emanations of some animals produce asthma and spasmodic cough in certain persons.

On moving the object glass they move with moderate activity, sometimes only quivering, sometimes forward and backward, shooting in the direction of their long axis; in a cooler temperature they are very sluggish. Sometimes they are in rows, side by side, as also in branched rows. Kept some days in the damp chamber they vegetate still more and become larger and more distinct than just after their discharge. It is to be remarked that only those secretions contain them which are discharged by strong sneezing, not that which flows out by drops. They seem to be firmly seated in the side-holes and recesses of the nose.

" When I received your first observations on the poisonous influence of quinine upon infusoria, I immediately determined to make an experiment, on the supposition that the described vibrios, if they were not the cause of the whole disease, they might, by their motions and products of decomposition, make it much more uncomfortable. For this purpose I made a saturated neutral solution of sulphate of quinia, which does not contain much of the salt (1.740), but is sufficiently active to produce a moderate burning of the nasal mucous membrane. I allowed about four centimetres to flow from a pipette into each nostril, while I lay upon my back with my nostrils turned upward. Then I moved my head to and fro that the fluid might flow about in all directions. When I stand upright the rest flows over the velum palati into the throat.

" The desired effect was immediate and continued for some hours. I could expose myself to the heat of the sun without an attack of sneezing and the other uncomfortable symptoms. The repetition, three times daily, of this application, sufficed to keep me free under the most unfavorable external circumstances. The vibrios then ceased in the secretion. If I only go out at evening an application before going out is sufficient. After a few days of treatment the symptoms ceased entirely ; if I omit the application the symptoms return again until the end of June approaches.

" The first experiment I made with quinine was in 1867 ; this year (1868) I have used it from the beginning, so soon as the first trace of the disease showed itself in May, and thereby succeeded in preventing its development.

"I have hitherto refrained from publishing this fact, because I had found no other patient upon whom I could try the experiment. Still I believe the very extraordinary regularity of the yearly return and yearly course of this disease, leaves no doubt that we have really to do with a very definite and quick influence of quinine upon the course of it; and this appears again to make my hypothesis very probable, that the vibrios living in the nasal secretions, although they may not be any indication of the specific character of the disease, and are of very frequent occurrence otherwise, still are the cause of the quick increase of the appearance in warm air, inasmuch as they are thereby aroused to greater activity."

Vibrios, similar to these figured and described in this letter, are very commonly observed in the nasal secretions, and are by no means in this country confined to any particular season of the year. If they infect the deep nasal

These reasons, although they are not without weight, cannot be admitted as sufficient to prove an animal origin of this disease.

GERM THEORY OF DISEASE.

§ 46. This theory may be called upon to afford an explanation of what cannot but be admitted to be a difficult matter. The relations of germs to disease, long ago suggested, was set forth many years since in this country by Dr. J. K. Mitchell, of Philadelphia, and has recently excited a good deal of discussion. It is certainly not improbable that germs (if we include under this indefinite term minute organisms both animal and vegetable) may be the cause of many forms of disease. Vegetables, like the oak, the cedar, and the rose, become diseased in consequence of the eggs deposited by insects. Flies, silk-worms, and other insects have upon and within their bodies various vegetable parasites; and some skin diseases of the human body are also believed to be caused by certain plants; in other cases, whether the plant is cause or effect, or simply an accompaniment, is not yet clearly shown.[1]

recesses, it is not easy to see how moderate changes in the temperature of the air could reach them; nor is it easy to see how an application of quinine to the nasal mucous membrane could poison vibrios in the eyes, which often suffer quite as much as the nose.

In Autumnal Catarrh the application of quinine in the manner proposed by Helmholtz for "Hay Fever," produced a good deal of irritation of the mucous membrane, but no relief of the symptoms.

[1] According to Hebra, the following diseases are caused by vegetable parasites : —

1. Favus, (a) Herpes tonsurans, (b) Pityriasis versicolor.

2. Alopecia arcata.

Isidor Neumann — Favus, Herpes tonsurans, Pityriasis versicolor.

Eczema marginatum, Nail fungus, Sycosis Parasitaria.

Nail fungus and favus may be the same. Kuchenmeister, *Manual of Parasites*, vol. ii. p. 220.

Eczema marginatum is only occasionally accompanied by fungus. I. Neumann, *Lehrbuch der Hautkrankheiten*, p. 403, Vienna, 1870.

Remak has proved that transplanted favus fungi will produce the disease in healthy skin.

These cryptogams are believed to be wafted about in the air as well as

Bacteria have been found in the human body in certain diseased conditions, but with regard to these much uncertainty exists.[1]

That germs of various kinds, both animal and vegetable, and in great quantity, may and do exist in the air, has been demonstrated. That some will bear the heat of boiling water and extreme cold,[2] and others be dried and transferred in other ways, and most frequently affect those in damp rooms on the north side of houses.

[1] Dr. Lionel S. Beall says (*Diseased Germ*, p. 63): "In every part of the body of man and the higher animals, and probably from the earliest age and in all stages of health, vegetable germs do exist. These germs are in a dormant or quiescent state, but may become active and undergo development during life, should the conditions favorable to their increase be manifested. Probably there is not a tissue in which these germs are not, nor is the blood of man free from them." P. 64.

Dr. Ferrier and Dr. Burdon Sanderson, F. R. S., at the meeting of the British Association at Edinburgh, 1871, read a paper *On the Origin and Distribution of Bacteria in Water, and the circumstances which determine their Existence in Animal Liquids and Fluids*. It is there stated, that "their examination of the fluids of the body tended to show that these, in their normal condition, did not contain the germs of *Bacteria* or other organisms."

Devaine, in 1864, discovered *Bacteria* in charbou or malignant pustule, in sheep; they have also been discovered in the same disease in man. For a time it was believed they were the sole causes of these diseases; it is now known that they exist in typhoid fever and common boils, and are not probably the cause of malignant pustule or any other disease, but simply one of the many effects of disease.

[2] Professor Wyman's experiments "on living organisms in heated water:" Exp. xv. Thirty-two flasks containing a boiled solution of "extract of beef," were arranged in six series, and boiled for different times, as seen in the following table: —

Series.	No. of Flasks in each Series.	Time Boiled.	Day on which Infusoria appeared.
		h. m.	
I.	5	0.30	1, 1, 2, 2, 2
II.	5	1.00	2, 2, 2, 2, 2
III.	5	1.30	1, 2, 2, 2, 2
IV.	5	2.20	2, 2, 3, 3, 2
V.	5	3.30 }	2, 2, 2, 4, 4, 4, 4
VI.	7	4.00 }	

From this it appears that infusoria appeared within four days after boil-

blown about in the atmosphere without losing their vitality, has also been proved.[1]   That some plants, like the
" Beer-plant of California," can be thoroughly dried, and
transported long distances, and yet, after a considerable
time, again produce their chemical effects, is well estab-
lished.   There is sufficient opportunity, therefore, for
these germs to reach the human body, and be drawn into
it through the mouth, the nose, or the eyes, or fall upon
the skin, and still retain their vitality.

ing four hours. "In pushing the experiments still further, we have not
found that infusoria appeared in any instance, if the boiling is prolonged to
five or six hours." — *American Journal of Science and Arts*, vol. xliv.,
September, 1867.

The lower kinds of algæ live in thermal springs, at 208° F.

The egg of the canker-worm will bear a temperature below zero, without
freezing or losing its vitality ; but if it be crushed at this temperature, it
immediately freezes.

[1] Drs. Ferrier and Sanderson still further report that "boiling the fluids
employed was always found to destroy all Bacteria and their germs; and
other experiments were recorded tending to show that the air did not contain living Bacteria, as so many have assumed. They also ascertained that
Bacteria were unable to resist the effects of desiccation even at the ordinary
temperature of the air."

These results as reported, are directly opposed to the experiments of
Professor Wyman. I quote the following experiment, one of many made
with reference to this question of the vitality of dried Bacteria : —

"*August* 3, 1871. In six similar vessels (all clean) was placed a weak solution of Liebig's extract of beef; they were all boiled five minutes. Dust
from dry packing straw, which had been a long time dry, was added to the
beef extract in three of the vessels ; the other three without addition were
kept as criteria. All were capped with paper and set upon a shelf equally
exposed to light and heat. *August 4th.* The three to which dust had been
added contained an abundance of vibrios, Bacteria, germinated spores of
mould, and some ciliated infusoria (Paramesium) ; the other three vessels
contained nothing. *August 5th.* Vibrios and Bacteria alone seen in the
vessels without dust ; in the other series, the infusoria mentioned above existed in still greater abundance."

From this it appears that Bacteria must have been added to the three
vessels, otherwise they would not have appeared in all of them so much
sooner than in the other three to which nothing had been added. That
these Bacteria had been and were still desiccated, is beyond doubt. If boiling kills Bacteria, then those which appeared in the other three vessels
must have been derived from the air in which, according to Dr. Sanderson's statement, they do not exist.

As to the assertion that certain vegetable organisms
have been found growing in profusion where intermittent
fever exists, and that this fever is not found where these
plants are wanting ; that it is the germs of these plants
which are the true cause of intermittents ; that measles in
the United States army was caused by a fungus in straw,
we can only say that the assertion has not been confirmed.[1] So also of the assertion that the germs of contagious diseases not only exist in the air, but have been
strained out of it, leaving a perfectly harmless atmosphere.[2] Until these statements, however confidently ex-

[1] Dr. J. H. Salisbury, in the *American Journal of Medical Sciences* for
January, 1866, states that he has found in the saliva of those suffering from
intermittents, certain species of palmellæ which grow in malarious soils,
and produce intermittents ; that they rise from the earth at night and fall in
the morning ; that where they are there is intermittent ; that the white
kind produces mild intermittent ; the red, congestive chill ; that they are
excreted in the urine and in the perspiration ; that a treatment founded on
the palmellæ is so successful that " a paroxysm never need occur after the
commencement of the remedies." As these and many other equally remarkable statements have not been confirmed either by Dr. S. or any other ob-
server, although it is more than five years since they were first published,
they are of little worth in this discussion.

Dr. Salisbury is also of opinion that measles is produced by the action
upon the human system of a peculiar fungus developed in decayed wheat-
straw, and cites an example. He also believes that he has produced measles
by inoculation with this fungus (*American Journal of Medical Sciences*, July,
1862). Dr. Woodward remarks that measles have broken out in camps
where no straw was used by the men, where they lay on cedar twigs or
India-rubber blankets, and where the sources of contagion could be traced.
It has prevailed in camp almost exclusively among those from the rural
districts, — those who as children had been most frequently exposed while
playing upon the straw ; for the fungus, a form of penicillum widely dif-
fused, is abundant in the grain stacks and in every stable where straw is
used for bedding. Attempts to repeat the experiments by inoculation
entirely failed in Dr. Woodward's hands, although he used the penicillum
produced as described by Dr. Salisbury, which microscopically was identical
with it. Dr. Salisbury's observations were made when measles were rife.
See J. J. Woodward, *On Camp Diseases*, p. 275.

Here also it must be admitted that more observations, more carefully
conducted, must be obtained before we can assent to the proposed theory.

[2] Dr. Tyndall, in a recent lecture on *Haze and Dust*, expresses his belief
confidently that the contagious element exists in the atmosphere in the

pressed, have been strengthened by more observations carefully made, we cannot admit the germ theory of disease as proved, however probable it may be.

As there is no more evidence that this theory explains the origin of Autumnal Catarrh than that of other diseases, it must be rejected here also.

§ 47. But even if it cannot be shown that germs recognizable by the microscope are connected with this disease, we are not therefore to infer that it is not excited by vegetable influences of some kind; for we know that several severe diseases or poisonings are so produced, where neither the microscopist nor the chemist can furnish any evidence of the cause.

§ 48. Is Autumnal Catarrh a "self-limited" disease? Has it a certain succession of processes, to be completed in a certain time; which time and processes may vary with the constitution and condition of the patient, but which are not known to be shortened or greatly changed by medical treatment?

form of germs. "As a planted acorn gives birth to an oak competent to produce a whole crop of acorns, each gifted with the power of reproducing its parent tree, and as thus from a single seedling a whole forest may spring, so these epidemic diseases literally plant their seeds, grow and shake abroad new germs which, meeting in the human body their proper food and temperature, finally take possession of whole populations." That this may be so cannot be denied, but it is safe to say there is as yet no proof of it whatever.

These germs and all other solid particles in the air, he assures us, can be strained out by means of "a handful of cotton wool," and the remaining air when examined with a beam of electric light, found to be "optically empty. The application of these experiments is obvious. If a physician wishes to hold back from the lungs of his patient, or from his own, the germs by which contagious disease is propagated, he will employ a cotton-wool respirator, I should be most willing to test their efficacy in my own person." — *Scientific Address*, by Prof. John Tyndall, New Haven, Conn., pp. 28–32.

If it can be shown that contagion or "contagious germs," with which Dr. T. tells us the air is filled, cannot act on the body through the skin or through the ears, or falling upon the eyes cannot be carried by the transparent fluid constantly flowing over these organs into the nostrils, and so into the throat, then it might be safe to trust to a protection which covers the mouth and nose only. Until then there is no safety in relying upon such contrivances.

Medical treatment limited to the use of drugs does not shorten or greatly change it ; medical treatment in its widest sense quickly and effectually breaks it up. It is, therefore, self-limited only when not properly treated. The same may be true of other diseases now so classed.[1]

---

[1] That certain diseases have a much more definite course and are less susceptible to medical treatment than others, has been long known. It was taught in the early part of this century by Pinel, one of the most philosophical of medical writers (*Nosographie Philosophique* — *Introduction*). Of late it has been pressed to a point where it seems to me there is danger of attaching to the expression "self-limited," ideas which may lead to carelessness or even fatalism in treatment. To this we oppose the following considerations : —

It must be remembered that diseases of the same name vary in the number, succession, severity, and duration of their processes in different epidemics to a degree that makes it difficult to recognize them. In the days of Sydenham, scarlet fever was "an ailment — we can hardly call it more." What therefore may be true of a disease in one epidemic may not be true of a disease of the same name in another.

. Although individual cases of all diseases which call for medical aid have been known to prove fatal, and death overtakes all at last, such cases are vastly outnumbered by those which terminate favorably under proper treatment.

With such variations we cannot assign the number, nor the succession of processes, nor the duration essential to a "self-limited" disease ; and even if we could, it would not be of great practical value, for in a large number of cases they are complicated with other evils giving them adventitious strength ; and of these, some, more formidable than the disease itself, are dependent upon circumstances under our control.

Erysipelas, classed as "self-limited," is a very different disease in its contagiousness, its processes, and termination in a long used, ill-ventilated hospital, from that treated in well-constructed buildings with pure air and healthy surroundings. The same may be said of hospital gangrene.

"If we divide with a cutting instrument the cellular or muscular tissue, we produce a self-limited disease." But whether this disease shall be cured by immediate union, union by the first intention, or union by granulation, each with its own succession of processes and duration, will often depend upon the hygienic conditions under which it is treated, whether in a crowded city hospital or in a well-constructed building with pure air in a healthy country.

Small-pox, also classed as self-limited, besides being prevented or modified by previous vaccination or inoculation, can be changed in the amount of eruption and consequent fever by treatment. Still further, we have the testimony of good observers, that during its stage of incubation when it

8

must be admitted to have by so far obtained foot-hold in the system, its severity and danger may even then be modified by vaccination.

Intermittent fever, formerly considered self-limited, can now with a good degree of certainty, be prevented, and in many cases even in its most fatal form, arrested. Autumnal Catarrh can be arrested in any stage by proper treatment.

Lastly, that diseases may be palliated and convalescence abridged by proper treatment, is admitted, or if not admitted, cannot be denied without abandoning the art of medicine itself.

Physiological actions and their modifications which constitute disease, are, under the influence of physical agents, so variable that we may well doubt if any class of diseases is of its own nature self-limited — it certainly has not been proved.

But even if nature has given to some diseases a more regular succession and duration of processes than others, we should no more neglect the art of medicine than agriculture should be neglected because nature has given to plants a certain period of growth and certain limits of excellence. Careful observation, experiment, and study have greatly changed the latter; there is good reason to believe it will lead to great benefits in the former. The classification of diseases as self-limited, although useful, must be held as provisional.

§ 49. THE necessity of means of recognizing this disease is obvious.

Its existence has been doubted, and still is doubted by many, even by physicians. The large number of cases here collected, and the details of symptoms given as much as possible, and at the risk of tedious repetition in the words of the patients themselves, especially when they are physicians, will, we think, leave no doubt in the minds of careful readers that it is a peculiar disease.

It is frequently misunderstood by patients who, notwithstanding its regular annual occurrence, have overlooked it, and supposed themselves suffering from a severe form of " common cold," arising from exposure during the changing weather of early autumn. Physicians, also, have confounded it with common catarrh, or considered it one of its modifications.

That it is worthy of a separate place in the descriptions of disease, is proved by the diagnostic symptoms, by which it can be readily recognized, and its course foretold.

Ordinary Catarrh — " *Common Cold.*" From this it can be distinguished by the peculiar redness and itching of the eyes, nose, and throat; by the profuse discharge; the successive invasion of different organs; the spasmodic cough and asthma towards its close; its regular annual return, its fixed time of disappearance; the readiness with which paroxysms are produced by certain irritants.

Bronchitis. The absence of headache, fever, and other signs of inflammation, and the predominance of symptoms connected with the eyes, nose, and throat. The absence of cough in the early stages; the absence of mucous and sibilant rales in the chest; its decided nervous symptoms; its regular annual return and disappearance.

Pneumonia. The absence of chills, headache, fever, and nasty expectoration; the affection of the eyes, nose, ears, and throat, with their violent itchings and profuse discharge; the absence of fine crepitus, bronchial respiration, bronchophony, dullness, and percussion; the usual physical signs; its annual return, its fixed time of continuance.

Local Inflammation of the Eyes — Conjunctivitis. By the violent paroxysmal itching of the internal canthi; the sudden and intense redness of the conjunctiva and its injected vessels, and its equally sudden disappearance. The absence of soreness, pain, and granulations; the puffiness of the eyelids. Generally, the great local disturbance compared with the slight constitutional disturbance. Later in the disease the edges of the lids are affected with small pustules.

June Cold of the Northern United States — " Hay Fever" (Catarrhus Æstivus of Dr. Bostock?). I have already remarked (p. 2), that those known to me as subjects of the June Cold of this country, and who were subsequently in England, or on the Continent, during the time they would have suffered here, did not suffer there.[1] This has left me in doubt as to the identity of the two diseases. As I have never seen a case of English " Hay

---

[1] Mrs. J. D. A. — Had June Cold many years in succession, but escaped the year she was in Europe, and also the year after her return; since then the attacks have again become regular.

Case 58. Mrs. J. B. — Escaped entirely her June Cold during the four years she was in England or on the Continent, although both before and after these years she suffered in the United States. Since the commencement of Autumnal Catarrh, in September, 1850, the June Cold, from which she had suffered annually for sixteen years, has very much diminished in severity and in length.

Fever," my comparison must be with the disease as it exists here.   Two cases are therefore given as examples.[1]

[1] The following are cases of the severer and milder forms of the "Rose Cold" or "June Cold" as it appears in this section of the United States — New England.

Miss S. J., of Cambridge, was born in Rhode Island and went to Cambridge when five years old.   So long as she can remember she has had a cold in summer; at other seasons she is uncommonly free from them.   She first noticed its connection with vegetation, roses especially, when eighteen years old.

The attack has commenced each year, for the past thirty years, about the 10th of June, or end of the first week in June, with watering of the eyes and nose, violent sneezing, sometimes compelling her to throw herself on the bed and so continue sneezing for several minutes; the nostrils are stuffed with a slimy adhesive mucus, sometimes with particles of blood, impeding respiration; throat dry and uncomfortable, but swallowing is not painful; great itching of the palate, throat, and ears, for relief of which the tongue is rubbed against the roof of the mouth and the fingers thrust into the ears.   There is also a sense of oppression in the head.   These symptoms usually continue throughout the disease.   The eyeballs have a sense of squinting; their movement is painful, but without swelling of the lids.

After a week there is a feeling of suffocation added to the other troubles, which continues till the third week, when cough commences with slight wheezing, very little expectoration, but the cough sometimes sufficiently severe to produce vomiting.   About the fifth week the sufferings all begin gradually to subside, the nasal troubles taking the lead, and by another week, the sixth from the commencement, the disease has disappeared.

The sense of suffocation is much relieved by going into the city of Boston, two miles distant, especially if the wind is east, but returns on leaving the city, even while upon the bridge over Charles River.   She is generally better during an east wind.   She was much more comfortable in Halifax, N. S., while living near the water.   Attar of roses or a fresh rose produces sneezing but not the other symptoms, and it soon ceases.   In going into a hayfield she has more than once been so affected as to become giddy and lose her sight, and been led out of the field, and on recovering go another way, avoiding the field and thereby escaping a paroxysm.   She has been obliged to leave a party where the room was dressed with flowers.   The hotter and brighter the weather, the more severe the disease; remaining in the dark greatly relieves her both as to eyes and nose.   The whole face is very sensitive; going into the sunshine will produce a paroxysm of sneezing, so will tickling the face with a hair.   She is always most comfortable with the windows closed.   The disease differs from an ordinary cold in its intervals of perfect relief for an hour or two.   Her father suffered severely from asthma.

My daughter, Mrs. C. F. Walcott, has always had good health and has

There are many points of resemblance between the two diseases. But they appear at different seasons of the year : the first in May and June, the second in August and September. Between these two periods, although I have made many inquiries, I can learn of no annually returning catarrh ; nor do I know of the first being prolonged into the period of the second. The June Cold is less severe, and of shorter duration ; the eyes are less severely, and less constantly affected. The cough is much less constant and not spasmodic, and asthma is less frequent at the close than in Autumnal Catarrh. Paroxysms of Autumnal Catarrh are seldom produced by new-mown hay, even when the grass is cut during the critical period ; nor are flowers so directly annoying. In June Cold, the new-mown hay is the most common cause of a paroxysm ; the aroma of flowers is also generally annoying. It is not generally relieved in mountainous regions, or in regions free from Autumnal Catarrh, but is decidedly relieved at the sea-side, and in large cities ; the reverse of what happens in the other disease.

Those who have June Cold are not subjects of Autumnal Catarrh. When June Cold has existed, it has ceased on the appearance of the later disease.[1] This,

been but little subject to ordinary cold. At twenty-two she began to suffer from catarrh during the cutting of grass in June and July. She is then seized with attacks of sneezing, obstruction of nostrils, and a flow of a thin limpid fluid, often requiring many handkerchiefs ; watering of the eyes and swelling of the eyelids. These attacks are in the order just stated, and last from fifteen minutes to an hour. They are excited by passing a hay-field, or in-doors if the cut hay is near by. They never occur at other seasons, when the grass is standing, or if it is cut, while still short and not in flower, either before or after the usual season, except once in September when passing a hay-field, during the cutting of the rowen or aftermath. She never suffers from the fragrance of roses or other flowers.

The disease is quite variable in severity in different years, and on the whole has of late become milder. She has now had eight annual returns.

For a description of the English form of the disease, by Dr. John Bostock, see the *Medico-Chirurgical Transactions*, vol. x. p. 161 ; vol. xiv. p. 437.

[1] Dr. Anson Hooker's case. — "Mrs. H. at the age of eighteen first no-

while it indicates a similarity between the two diseases, indicates also that there is probably a specific difference, in analogy with what we see in two similar but not identical eruptive febrile diseases.

These three questions, affirmatively answered, will usually determine the diagnosis, —

1. Has the patient had several similar attacks ?

2. Have they occurred annually at the critical period : August 15th—September 25th ?

3. Have they ceased, or been relieved by change of residence ?

ticed that she was affected by the aroma of roses. The following year, while picking roses in the morning, had itching of the eyes, which became so intolerable by afternoon that she asked medical advice. After this she could not be in a room with many flowers without affection of the eyes and catarrhal symptoms. This state of things continued about ten years, when she began to have her regular Autumnal Catarrh, and the sensitiveness to flowers very materially decreased, but has not entirely disappeared."

Case 40. — The yearly attack formerly commenced in June ; now it commences between August 20th and 27th, and terminates September 10th to 20th.

Case 65. Mrs. M. — At sixteen had catarrh commencing in June and ending about July 4th or during haying time. This occurred annually for seventeen years. Five years ago after some irregularity in its period of termination it ceased altogether, and a catarrh appeared about August 1st, when near Fall River, Mass. The three subsequent years she was in Oregon, Illinois, where it appeared August 17th, and this year (1866) while in Charlestown, Mass., August 24th.

Case 11. — Mr. E. F. Atkins at ten years of age had attacks of catarrh when in a field of new-mown hay, lasting two hours after leaving the field, with itching and watering of the eyes for an hour longer. About the same age he began to have catarrhal attacks commencing about August 20th, and continuing till the last week in September. These have been repeated to the present time, but the first attacks are much less severe.

Mrs. H. T. M., of Cambridge, at fourteen was attacked with a catarrh in June, which recurred annually for eight years. She then became affected with watering of the eyes and obstruction of the nostrils, sneezing, and a copious discharge of watery fluid. This commences annually August 18th, and disappears with frost. Since the commencement of the catarrh, which has now continued twelve years, has had no recurrence of the June Cold.

§ 50. DIFFERENTIAL DIAGNOSIS.

COMMON COLD.

No itching of eyes, nose, or throat.

Slight lachrymation.

Sneezing moderate, not in paroxysms.

Conjunctiva slightly injected; no sudden attacks of redness.

No spasmodic cough; no asthma.

No annual return.

Not influenced by change of place.

AUTUMNAL CATARRH.

Violent itching of eyes, nose, and throat.

Profuse lachrymation, and profuse discharge from nostrils.

Violent and prolonged sneezing in paroxysms.

Conjunctiva very red; vessels much injected in paroxysms; sudden in attack and disappearance.

Cough spasmodic; asthma.

Regula rannual return about August 15th; disappearing September 25th–30th.

Entire relief in certain places.

ACUTE BRONCHITIS.

Headache, fever, signs of inflammation.

No itching of eyes, nose, or throat; no profuse discharge.

No violent sneezing.

Appetite diminished.

No annual return.

Not sensitive to certain plants.

Mucous rales.

Asthma rare.

No set time of disappearance.

AUTUMNAL CATARRH.

No headache, or very slight; no fever.

Violent and sudden attacks of itching of eyes, nose, and throat; profuse limpid discharge from nose and eyes.

Violent and long continued sneezing.

Appetite good.

Annual return at critical period.

Paroxysms produced by certain plants.

No mucous rales.

Asthma common towards end.

Disappears about last of September.

JUNE CATARRH OF NORTHERN UNITED STATES.	AUTUMNAL CATARRH.
Time of annual attack : May, June.	Time of annual attack : August, September.
Affection of eyes moderate, throat occasionally sore.	Affection of eyes, nose, and throat, severe.
Edge of eyelids not inflamed.	Edge of eyelids inflamed.
Eyelids not puffy.	Eyelids puffy.
Cough not spasmodic.	Cough spasmodic.
Asthma not common.	Asthma common towards close.
No itching of skin, no eruption.	Itching of skin, with eruptions slow in healing.
Generally much relieved at the sea-coast, and in large cities.	Rarely relieved at the sea-coast, or in large cities.
Paroxysms generally produced by new-cut hay, and by the aroma of flowers.	Paroxysms not produced by new-cut hay; seldom produced by the aroma of flowers.
Not relieved in mountains.	Entire relief in certain regions.

§ 51. It varies somewhat in severity in successive years. In early life the first attacks are often as severe as any subsequent ones; in other instances they gradually increase in severity as age advances ; [1] in a few it has pretty steadily diminished, and even become perfectly bearable, but it has not disappeared.[2] I know of no signs which will enable us to predict its courses in this respect. It does not seem

[1] The four cases which follow all show an increase of severity as the attacks multiply : —

Case 58. — The cough and asthma have of late years continued longer, and even into the winter. The disease gradually assumed the form of chronic bronchitis, from which after several years she died. The last two years of her life she escaped the catarrh by change of residence.

Case 60. Dr. Derby. — She thinks the disease has increased in severity during the past few years; as a girl she had no cough.

Case 68. — " The annual attacks are increasing in severity."

Case 19. — " I think my annual attack increases in severity and with more feeling of soreness about the chest."

[2] *Case* 7. Dr. J. C. Hayden. — " I suffer less from the disease than I did in former years, and find that it commences later."

Case 67. — " The attacks are becoming less severe, although she passes the months of August and September in Cambridge."

Case 61. Mrs. S. B. Bradford. — " For the first eight or ten years the attacks were most severe; they have gradually been diminishing in severity the last ten years, but so gradually that I can hardly fix upon a precise period when they became less severe. But for the last year (1864–65) or two I hardly notice that I have more than a simple cold."

Case 6. — Dr. Lyman's second case would indicate that the disease has been modified since the first attack; it commenced at four years of age with asthmatic symptoms of great severity, and at eighteen had nearly disappeared. The case, however, is peculiar in several respects, and may have been of a different character from true Autumnal Catarrh.

Samuel Batchelder, Esq. — " I think it has gradually diminished in severity for many years past, but it is quite as regular in the time and duration of its attacks."

to bear any relation to age, sex, strength, make of body, or health.

It may be assumed that the predisposition once developed into a full attack, will continue in a greater or less degree, through life. I have never yet met with a case in which it has failed to make its annual appearance so long as a patient remained in a catarrhal region. Instances are on record of persons arriving at .extreme old age without escape.

The changes most likely to follow many repetitions are those affecting the nasal mucous membrane ; a sensitiveness and an inclination to turgidity of the tissues, which are very apt to occur, independently of the causes usually producing catarrh. Similar changes occur in the bronchial mucous membrane, accompanied by a continuance of cough into the winter, which if they do not actually produce attacks of bronchitis generally aggravate them.[1] There is also a tendency to, what seems to me, a nervous disturbance of the heart, producing palpitation and irregularity, which may have an influence upon one who has been the subject of rheumatism or cardiac trouble from other causes.

Such results are quite rare ; the great majority suffer only at the annual return. Indeed, there is evidence that the critical period once passed, very many persons are less subject than most people, during the remainder of the year, to attacks of bronchitis and catarrh from ordinary causes. Some even go further, and assert that they believe themselves less liable to other diseases than most persons. This belief has possibly some foundation in truth, and may be admitted as evidence that the disease does not materially impair the general health.

The influence on longevity is a matter of interest to the

---

[1] *Case* 59. — In 1859 apparently took cold from exposure just as the disease was disappearing, which produced an increase and continuance of the cough, for which she went to Savannah, Ga., where it disappeared in about six weeks.

life insurance companies. To them a cough is a serious
matter, and asthma usually brings with it an increased
premium, whatever be its cause; so, also, of a constant
or frequently recurring catarrh. A medical examiner, not
aware of the nature of the disease, may well hesitate with
regard to a sufferer in the midst of an attack during the
spasmodic stage, with its cough and asthma existing at
times for years, and moreover a family trouble. Indeed,
I have known a case abruptly closed on the statement of
these two facts alone. In such cases, a more experienced
and more critical examination might secure to the offices
the insurance of lives which would prove valuable to
them.

Autumnal Catarrh, although it has the tendencies just
mentioned, has but little influence generally, either of
itself or its complications, in shortening life. There are
many instances of exceptionally long lives among those
who are and have long been subjects of the disease.

Daniel Webster, a subject for twenty years to the last
year of his life, died at seventy; Chief Justice Shaw at
eighty; another gentleman at eighty-four; and Samuel
Batchelder is now eighty-seven, and thinks the attacks less
severe than formerly. One lady, now eighty-one, has had
it many years, and another died at seventy-nine, having
suffered most of her life. An inspection of the table will
show that twenty years is a very common duration.

The history of the disease, while it affords a pretty
good prospect of a life-long periodical suffering, promises
for the intervals, good health, and gives the comfortable
assurance that it does not materially shorten life.

§ 52. My principal object in this paper is to give, as far as possible, the natural history of Autumnal Catarrh. To the sufferer, the most important inquiry is how it can be prevented or relieved. I think it must be admitted that a knowledge of its natural history has in this respect led to valuable results.

It must be borne in mind that the disease appears at a certain time, has a definite course, and terminates in all at about the same period, notwithstanding great differences in circumstances and modes of treatment. We infer, therefore, that in these respects it is very little under the influence of *medicines*. Indeed, no well authenticated case has come to my knowledge in which the disease has been broken up in the midst of its career, or its annual return prevented by the use of medicines. This does not prove that specific remedies do not exist; but inasmuch as the disease is a bearable one, it is not worth while, with our present knowledge, to run great risks of life, or permanently deranged health, in pursuit of an object which, at best, is of doubtful attainment.[1]

[1] *Case* 8. Daniel Webster. — In 1851, while in the White Mountains during the usual period of catarrh, he was prevailed upon by a clergyman who seems to have suffered from " Hay Asthma," to try a variety of remedies, among which were iodide of potassium, blue pills, Rochelle powders, iron, potash, and arsenic, until Mr. Webster says, " My system is so full of iron, potash, and arsenic, that my stomach has become deranged." " By the process I have lost flesh and am not a little reduced."

September 8th he again writes, " I have had rather a hard time. I have been able to keep off the catarrh so far, but it has called on me to take so much medicine as a good deal to derange my system." He left Franklin and the White Mountain region and arrived in Boston September 15th, and was at once attacked. The polypharmacy was immediately discontin-

Fortunately, the study of the natural history of the disease has shown us a remedy which is successful in all its periods, — a removal to a non-catarrhal region. These regions, so far as known, have been defined in § 8.

This is the great, not to say the only remedy.

For complete prevention, the place of refuge should be reached a day or two before the usual time of attack, especially if the journey is by rail in hot, dry, and dusty weather; for this combination is very apt to hasten an outbreak. If the disease has already commenced, relief can be obtained within forty-eight hours, and frequently sooner, after arrival. If it is far advanced, and local changes are produced, — inflamed eyes, nose, throat, and air tubes, — these effects will remain for a longer or shorter period, according to their severity, or the general health. It is not safe to return to any catarrhal region

ued by his usual medical adviser, Dr. Jeffries. Besides the derangements of the system, this treatment was otherwise unfortunate; it probably prevented his discovery that he owed his relief, up to that time, not to drugs, but to his residence meanwhile at the White Mountains and Franklin.

Case 76. — " One year, in September, I got iodide of potassium and syrup of tolu, and it seemed to operate as a specific for that year, but has failed ever since. I have tried most all the remedies known to the physicians of the various kinds of practice, such as burning saltpetre paper, smoking stramonium leaves, cigars, pennyroyal leaves, belladonna, *lobelia emelias*, chloroform, ether, morphine, and iodide of potassium; the last two, perhaps, have been of service. Most of these medicines seem more to divert the mind than to afford any specific relief."

Case 16. — " I have been under homœopathic treatment, taken aconite and nux vomica and other things unknown to me, without relief."

Case 19. — " I have tried various remedies. I was under the care of a homœopath, who gave me little powders in September; they did me no good; nor am I aware that any other treatment has done me good."

Case 4. — " I have been treated by several different physicians during the many years I have suffered from catarrh, among them homœopaths, without other than very temporary relief."

Case 67. — " I have taken homœopathic remedies without relief; so of the inhalation of ether and other remedies.

My inquiries have always been directed to the treatment, and the answers are so clear as to the persistence of the disease, that further evidence upon that point is unnecessary.

north of New York until the last week of September, or until after two or three killing frosts ; those who are very sensitive, should not return until the first of October. To places south of New York as far as Richmond, beyond which our observations do not extend, return should be delayed until the middle or third week of October, or until frost in those places.

A compliance with these conditions will secure, with very rare exceptions, complete immunity from the disease.

§ 53. *Preventive Treatment.* Although we know of no medicines upon which we can rely for entire prevention, by their help the system can be put in a better condition for meeting the enemy. In this, as in other chronic affections (for we must suppose a peculiar condition which exists during the intervals of the attacks), the main object should be to build up the system. Dietetic measures, therefore, in the widest sense, are of more value than medicines, although these, too, are useful.

As the disease has more of a general than local character, and affects more deeply the nervous system than the mucous membrane, more is to be expected from constitutional than local treatment. More, also, is to be expected from mild measures than from those that are stormy, and almost necessarily debilitating.

Few diseases are so peculiarly individual in their character, hence no one method can be suited to all cases. Each is to be studied by itself; and as it is not subject to sudden and dangerous changes, time and opportunity are given for observation and experiment, and the patient may become, to a great extent, his own physician.

Great heat, and the direct rays of the sun, are to be avoided; they have a depressing influence upon the nervous system ; and if extreme, and combined with fatigue, are of themselves dangerous. In a moderate degree they lessen the powers of resistance. Avoid the smoke and
of the railway, and the dust of the street. Close the

windows of the sleeping-room early in the afternoon, and keep them closed through the night; the movement of the air is annoying, and still air allows the subsidence of particles which are believed to be injurious.

The diet should be nourishing. Abstinence from animal food reduces the strength and aggravates the symptoms. Alcoholic stimulants do not defer the attack, and, so far as my own observations extend, are rather a detriment. Various experiments have been made on the quantity of liquids drank, on the supposition that they may modify the flow from the nose and eyes. Abstinence for many days in succession did not diminish it, nor was it increased by an excessive use of liquids.

The sensitiveness of the skin is so noticeable, that cold bathing and cold shower-baths have been used to harden it, but without marked success, except so far as they are agreeable. Many persons, especially the subjects of Autumnal Catarrh, bear cold shower-bathing badly; the system does not react, and they remain a long time chilled.

Warm clothing; flannel next the skin during the month of August, and increased while the disease is in progress, is of great importance.[1] It protects from sudden changes of temperature to which the skin is peculiarly sensitive, and with which the nervous system at this time has a close sympathy. Rubbing with a flesh brush is also of service.

---

[1] *Case* 20. W. H. Y. Hackett, Esq. — "I was for several years under medical treatment and no advantage. I have long since made up my mind to use no medicines; but use such alleviating agents as experience has shown to be beneficial.

"As soon as I am attacked I put on flannel waistcoat and drawers. I find riding in the railway train very injurious; am better near the sea than in the country. I sometimes get relief by holding my face over boiling water — taking a cup of hot tea or coffee — sitting in a warm room. One year I was quite comfortable from washing the body in warm water in which pearlash had been dissolved, and then covering the body with sweet oil. The last year it did not do so well. The difficult breathing in the night is relieved by whiskey and a bottle of boiling water to my feet. I have sometimes found relief from a warm bath. A generous diet, and whatever keeps up the system, is apparently beneficial." ·

The application of sweet oil to the whole surface, after it has been thoroughly washed in a solution of soda or pearlash, or other alkaline carbonate, is reported to have been useful. This also protects the skin from change of temperature.

Of medicines as preventives, many have been recommended. Among these are quinine, iron, arsenic, strychnine, and nux vomica, iodide of potassium, bromide of potassium, hydrocyanic acid, and wild cherry bark infusion. Nearly all of these have an influence upon the nervous system. It is very difficult to determine the value of any of these substances; the number of cases in which each has been tried, is too small to draw any definite conclusion. This much, however, may be said, that few persons are so well satisfied with the results of any one treatment as to repeat it from year to year.

Quinine may be excepted from this statement. It appears to have been more successful than the other remedies; it has been tried by several persons for successive years, with similar results. It is known to be a specific in intermittent fever, and by analogy may be supposed to do good in this regularly returning affection. It is a good tonic, and increases the desire for food, and the ability to digest and appropriate it. Its use should be commenced at least a fortnight before the critical period, in doses of two grains with each meal, and continued through the disease. It has been used in large doses, producing ringing of the ears, and deafness in one case, without advantage. Arsenic, in the form of Fowler's solution, has also evidence in its favor. It should be taken with care, and under medical ... ; the dose need not exceed three or four drops with

...e bowels should be moved daily. Gentle laxatives, Congress water, Rochelle powders, citrate of magne-: a rhubarb pill, are useful. Violent purging should oided.

If the secretions of the kidneys are deficient in quantity, or dark colored, the occasional use of bitartrate of potash (cream of tartar), as a drink, is advisable.

§ 54. *Palliative Measures.* So many remedies are praised as sure cures for the various symptoms, by one or another, that we might well wonder that any allow themselves to suffer at all, were it not that these same remedies entirely fail with others. The natural remissions of the disease are such that even the wary and experienced are often deceived into the hope, not destined to be realized, that it is really taking its leave ; while the sanguine are happy in the belief that the last new remedy has achieved a victory. Still, a certain degree of relief is obtained by remedies.

§ 55. Local applications are useful. Protecting the eyes from strong light by colored spectacles or goggles, or sitting in a dark room, gives considerable relief; bathing them with cold water, or ice-water, or covering them with cold, wet cloths, relieves the burning. Others, again, find relief in tepid bathing of the face and eyes. When a paroxysm of itching comes on, refrain from rubbing them ; it produces a different irritation, which disappears more slowly than that of the disease. Avoid accesses of sneezing as much as possible ; it is the beginning of trouble in both nose and eyes. If the eyelids are inflamed, the edges should be slightly smeared with " cold cream," or other mild ointment. Some relief to the irritated conjunctiva is obtained from washing the eyes in an infusion of chamomile tea, or by the use of a mild sedative solution of biborate of soda (borax), five or six grains to an ounce of camphor water, a popular remedy with oculists.

The discharge from the nostrils may be relieved by the " head bath; " holding the head over a bowl of very hot milk and water, or hot water alone, while the head and shoulders are covered with a thick shawl; it produces a copious perspiration. Blowing the nose should be avoided as much as possible; it increases the obstruction and discomfort. Let the limpid fluid be wiped away with a soft handkerchief; it will then sooner cease. In railway travelling, considerable protection is given by small pieces of sponge dipped in water and placed just within the nostrils; they exclude dust and smoke, and interfere not at all with breathing. A veil of Swiss muslin, wet with water, is a still more complete protection to the whole face.

The nostrils are often completely obstructed early in the morning; active exercise, running up-stairs, or energetic movements of the body and limbs, of any kind, which sends the blood to the extremities, will give immediate temporary relief, and enable one who can hardly swallow, to eat a breakfast with comfort. Hot whiskey and water, before leaving the bed in the morning, is said to prevent attacks of sneezing and closed nostrils. Various irritants have been recommended for the relief of the nostrils; camphor and sugar finely powdered, and used as snuff; cayenne pepper, water of ammonia, held under the nose, and the vapor inhaled. Dropping a solution of quinine into the nostrils, as recommended by Helmholtz in " June Cold," is not known to have succeeded in this disease.

At night the body should be warmly covered; perspiration is desirable. The windows should be closed, and all drafts avoided. If the patient can take opium without inconvenience, five or ten grains of Dover's powder, or the equivalent in laudanum or morphine, at bed-time, will render the night much more comfortable. In the daytime, an hour in bed, warmly covered, will give great relief to severe paroxysms.

Gargling the throat with a solution of a teaspoonful of chlorate of potash in a pint of cold water, and the chewing of cubeb peppers, relieves the itching.

For the relief of spasmodic cough, morphine in doses of one sixth of a grain, fluid extract of hyoscyamus, and tincture of Indian hemp, are used. Bromide of potassium and hydrate of chloral relieve the accompanying nervous symptoms. The various soothing household remedies — flax-seed tea, gum arabic solution, or bits of the gum dissolved in the mouth, and swallowed, are not to be rejected for temporary relief.

§ 56. *Asthma.* Like all nervous affections, this also yields to a great variety of means, sometimes the most opposite. Most require fresh air in large quantity, others seek a hot room, hot foot-baths, and copious perspiration. Experience alone teaches what will relieve, hence the various trials and observations of patients lead to a course sometimes more successful than that prescribed by physicians.

Of all the remedies, the smoking of stramonium leaves has been most successful. They may be dried and smoked in a pipe, or broken up and made into cigarettes, or burned in the room. But they do not relieve all. A secret remedy, much used, is composed of powdered stramonium leaves and salpetre in the proportion of three parts of the first to one of the last; the powder is placed in small conical heaps, burned, and the smoke inhaled. The Espic cigarettes are often used; each cigarette contains the following substances : —

℞ Belladonna leaves	. . . . .	$4\frac{1}{2}$ grains.
Hyoscyamus leaves	. . . . .	$2\frac{1}{4}$ grains.
Stramonium leaves	. . . . .	$2\frac{1}{4}$ grains.
Phellandrium aquaticum leaves	. .	$\frac{3}{4}$ grain.
Opium	. . . .	$\frac{1}{6}$ grain.

Mix. These are powdered, carefully mixed, and rolled up in paper. Only two cigarettes should be smoked during a single attack; used to excess, they cease to give relief.

Saltpetre paper is a popular remedy. The paper is dipped in a half-saturated solution of saltpetre, dried, and rolled into cigarettes, and smoked or burned in the room. The inhalation of the vapor of water of ammonia

through the mouth, with the nostrils closed, frequently succeeds. A teaspoonful should be poured into a bowl, and
the face held a foot or two above it; the inhalation to be
continued a quarter of an hour.

Arsenical cigarettes, to be found at the apothecaries, are
frequently smoked with relief. They should be used with
care, a few puffs at a time.

The inhalation of sulphuric ether and chloroform give
relief to some; in such cases the relief is usually immediate; it should not be pushed to insensibility. The inhalation of carbolic acid has been useful.

The treatment may be summed up as follows: —

1. *Remain in a non-catarrhal region during the critical
period.*

2. Strengthen the system by food and tonics.

3. Avoid dust, smoke, night air, and the vicinity of
plants known to produce a paroxysm.·

4. Dress warmly, with flannels next the skin.

5. For the cough, mild narcotics: various household
demulcents.

6. For asthma: smoking stramonium leaves, saltpetre,
Espic cigarettes, arsenical cigarettes, inhalation of sulphuric
ether, carbolic acid.

ILLUSTRATIVE CASES.

§ 57. The following cases will give a full and accurate account of the disease as it appears in different individuals. They contain many facts in a connected manner, which could not be presented in the Tabular View : —

CASE 10.

Author's Case. — My first attack of Autumnal Catarrh was in 1833, the year of my graduation from Harvard University, at the age of twenty-one. From that time it has returned annually, commencing about the 20th of August, not varying a week from that date, and of late years more regularly about the 24th, and continuing until the last week in September, or until one or two killing frosts.

It begins with an itching in the inner corners of the eyes and in the internal ear and throat. This is soon followed by watering of the eyes, with irritation, and a limpid and profuse discharge from the nose. That from the eyes is excessive, and flows over the lids ; both require the almost constant use of a handkerchief. In a day or two paroxysms of sneezing and nose-blowing occur ; not an ordinary sneeze ; it is more violent, and many follow in quick succession. The nostrils are obstructed, one or both at times completely closed. Generally this obstruction is of short duration, coming on suddenly and as suddenly going off ; at other times, as in the morning before breakfast, it is often prolonged, and materially interferes with swallowing. But what is very singular, however completely the nostrils are shut up, they are at once opened for the time by any exercise which gives warmth to the extremities, running, or active movements of any kind. The attacks of itching in the eyes are frequent and very annoying ; the vessels of the conjunctiva are enlarged, and if irritated by rubbing (and the tendency to rub them is almost irresistible), the surface becomes of a nearly uniform red. This redness soon disappears. The affections of the eyes, nose, and throat, come on in fits, and are most severe morning and evening. They are aggravated by dust and smoke, especially when combined, as in railway travelling, and by the evening air. The eyes are sensitive to light ; the lids are inflamed and tender ; the edges have not unfrequently small pustules, which are quite painful, and continue several days. I am better in rainy weather than in fair weather, partly because of the absence of dust, but also, I think, the absence of other noxious influences.

The itching of the internal ear is often very annoying, causing attempts at relief by rubbing the external surface with the point of my finger. The throat also suffers in the same way, and the tongue is pressed and rubbed against the roof of the mouth for relief. These attempts, however, avail but little.

The skin itches, especially on the back between the shoulders, and on the scalp. It is sensitive to slight irritation; the cuticle is easily removed, and does not readily reform; and not unfrequently eruptions appear, principally in the armpits, which also heal slowly.

The difficulty of breathing through the nostrils, and the sudden chokings from dryness of the throat, make the nights restless, and cause dreams of impending suffocation. To these is added a peculiar nervous condition difficult to describe, which compels to frequent change of position, or even quitting the bed for relief.

This state of things continues a week or ten days, with varying and deceptive severity, every little while diminishing and raising a hope that the disease is disappearing, and then returning in full force. A cough now comes on, frequent, irritative, and without expectoration. After a time it becomes paroxysmal, most severe in the night, compelling me to sit up in bed, and frequently causing retching and attempts to vomit. Even after many minutes of severe coughing, the only expectoration is a little transparent mucus, which brings but slight relief. These attacks make the muscles of the chest sore, and exhaust both by their violence and by the loss of sleep.

I have some wheezing in the breathing at night after these severe attacks of coughing, but never decided asthma.

During this stage of the disease, the system suffers, the appetite is lessened, and both flesh and strength are diminished. The vigor and inclination to effort, mental or physical, is also less, with a general sensitiveness to annoying external impressions. The action of the heart becomes excited and intermitting, occasioning much discomfort after exercise.

At the commencement of the third week, the disease begins to diminish. The fits of sneezing are less frequent and shorter during the day, and are soon confined to the early morning; the secretion from the nostrils is thicker, and not so irritating; the eyes are better, neither so sensitive to the light, nor so tearful; the paroxysms of cough lessen in frequency and severity; the expectoration is increased, is thicker and more satisfactory. By the last week in September, or after a good frost, it entirely disappears.

My first attack was while in Cambridge; afterwards I was in Boston and the immediate vicinity until 1837; since then in Cambridge.. In all these places the attacks have been equally severe, unless it be that I gained some relief by passing the day at the rocky peninsula of Nahant, where I escaped heat and dust. In 1865 I spent my usual period of suffering in the White Mountain region, principally at Gorham and in the Glen. While in these parts I was free from the disease. I have also tried various other places, the Profile House, Littleton, Lancaster, Crawford House, but in none of them have I been so free as in the Glen. At Grand Monadnock I got no relief. Three seasons have been passed under canvass on the banks of the Peabody, with complete relief. One year, 1869, I was in the Highlands of Scotland, also quite well.

So long as I remained at home, the disease did not, I think, diminish in severity; on the other hand, with later years, I have been weaker, and my strength is regained more slowly; neither have my visits to the mountains for four successive years lessened the tendency to it. Several years I have not sought the White Mountains until the signs of disease were obvious; and a year ago I was detained until the second of September, when the severity was as in former years. The functional disturbance of the heart, after my visit to the mountains, ceased.

Medical treatment has availed little even in diminishing its severity. This is probably because I cannot take opium or morphine, even in small quantity. I have been benefited by warm flannels next the skin during the critical period, and a generous diet of meat and vegetables. Wine and other stimulants have done me no good. I avoid all irritants, dust, and smoke, during the day, and the evening air. The windows of my sleeping-room are closed early in the afternoon, and kept closed through the night. I avoid blowing my nose as much as possible, as it almost inevitably produces complete obstruction of the nostrils.

My father suffered from a similar and probably the same disease. Of his four sons and a daughter, all who arrived at maturity, three sons and the daughter are affected; my own son is a sufferer, and my daughter has June Cold.

CASE 8.

Hon. Daniel Webster. — The private correspondence of this eminent statesman shows clearly that he was a subject of Autumnal Catarrh.

The first attack was in 1832, when about fifty years old, and while living in Boston. It commenced usually about the 23d of August, and ended about the 1st of October. August 15, 1849, he writes, "In seven days I shall begin to sneeze and blow my nose; and the first week the catarrh is usually most severe." The eyes were first attacked. Sept. 12, 1850: "I use the confidential hand of another to write you a short letter, my eyes holding out to perform a small part of the duty expected of them every day. I am in the midst of my periodical catarrh, or 'hay fever,' or whatever you please to call it. I read nothing, and hardly write anything but signatures. The disease is depressing and discouraging. I know there is no remedy for it, and that it must have its course. One misfortune is, I cannot take, even in the smallest quantity, the common remedy, opium. It produces loss of appetite and great prostration of strength ; but since the event of last week terminated, I have some little time for rest, and shutting myself up very much, I keep as quiet as I can." Again : "My annual cold is now heavy upon me, weakening my body and depressing my spirits. It has yet a fortnight to run ; and perhaps will sink me lower than it did when strong excitement enabled me to withstand it. I have lost a good deal of flesh, and you will think me thin and haggard. I have had little sleep, not four hours a night on an average, for the whole six months." This was immediately after the passage of the "fugitive slave law."

Sept. 18 : "My head and eyes are not in the best condition. Travelling against a strong wind has brought on my cold badly, and to-day I am not well. The cold, or influenza, with which I am lately visited, is likely, according to former experience, to last some weeks, and quite disables me from public speaking." 1845, at Marshfield, the attack seems to have been earlier than usual. " Here, August 17, I have been more or less under the influence of my incurable catarrh. Some days I have felt quite discouraged. Now it seems a little better. The paroxysms are not so frequent, though two days ago I had a very bad forenoon. It came on in a moment, and went off, when it did go, just as quick. Some days I feel quite well, and can keep out without inconvenience, if the weather be fair ; on other days I cannot go out at all, fair or foul. Last Thursday was fair weather. I went over to the Gurnet, and caught some fish, and felt well all day. Since then my catarrh has been continually quite severe. I hope it will soon begin to taper off."

Oct. 4, 1851, at Marshfield : "The catarrh, with its sneezing, its nose-blowing, its cough, and its asthma, seems to be taking leave. My eyes are still weak, but my greatest difficulty at present is a general want of strength."

The following year, 1852, also at Marshfield, Sept. 12 : "The catarrh is upon me in its various forms, alternating as usual, but as yet not so severe and heavy as on former occasions. My general health is not so much prostrated. If the weather be wet or damp, I must stay in the house, and have a little fire to prevent fits of sneezing and nose-blowing. When the sun is very bright, I am obliged to avoid going out on account of my eyes, except, indeed, when the sea is calm, and I am protected by an awning. The bracing air of the ocean I feel very beneficial."

Nov. 5, 1850. While Secretary of State, Mr. Webster, evidently under the influence of his depressing malady, writes to the President : " I am quite aware how inconvenient my long absence is to you and the government, and sometimes I feel that as this illness is of annual occurrence, I ought to regard it as unfitting me for an office the duties of which require constant attention ; I must now go to Marshfield for a few days. When there a fortnight ago, I was hardly able to go out of doors, and could do nothing about arranging my little affairs."

Sept. 28, at Marshfield : " Sometimes the force of the catarrh seems pretty much broken, and then it returns, attacking the head, eyes, nose, etc., with great violence. I think it is approaching its last stage, which is the asthmatic stage. Some of our friends who are subjects of the complaint, and have short necks, dread this. I do not fear much from this, although in this stage I feel its influence more or less on the chest. In such a day as this, a northeast rain storm pouring, I cough a little, and am as hoarse as a frog." Oct. 4 : " The recent weather, cold for the season, has been useful to me."

The previous year, Sept. 27 : " My catarrh is going off, or else is having a long intermission ; and for whichever it may be, I am truly thankful."

Sept. 29, 1848, at Marshfield : " My catarrh is greatly relieved. If I get through the night without a paroxysm, I mean to set the lark an example of early rising to-morrow, and listen to the ' murmurs of the Atlantic surge ' before the sun fairly purples the east."

Some years it lasted longer. 1850, Oct. 14 : " Tuesday, the 8th, I was to have gone into State Street to meet the people, but I did not find myself well enough. The next day, Wednesday, I came down to my house a good deal sick, and have hardly been out of doors from that day to this. My catarrh has held on unaccountably, and for three or four days I was quite ill with it, so much so that I called a physician."

Mr. Webster, during the critical period, was in successive years in Washington, New York, Boston, and at his sea-side residence in Marshfield, near Plymouth, Mass. In all these places he suffered nearly equally. In 1839, he was in Scotland during the month of August, and the greater part of September, and was exposed to the rain at Lord Eglintoun's tournament, but escaped entirely.

In 1849, August 30, he was in Franklin, N. H., about forty miles south of the Mount Washington region. " My cold was severe coming up in the ' cars,' but since Monday evening I have hardly felt it. My eyes are weak, and I am obliged to avoid the sun ; but so far I have suffered nothing in comparison with former years."

In 1851, August 6 : " To-morrow I think of going to New Hampshire, hardly so much for a change of air as to look after some private affairs. In general I find that those affected by my complaint avoid the interior and come to the coast. But this is not universal." Franklin, N. H., August 10 : " I came to these regions on the morning of Thursday the 7th, thinking that the mountain air might strengthen me against the times when I expect my enemy, the catarrh, to attack me." August 19 : " Although I date this letter from Franklin, N. H., I write it among the White Mountains. I stayed at Franklin until the railway trains, passing and repassing every few hours, began to bring me many daily visitors ; and as I wished for quiet and privacy, I took my own conveyance and came off in this direction. I have never had confidence that I should be able to avert entirely the attack of catarrh ; but I believe that at least I shall gain so much in general health and strength as to enable me in some measure to resist its influence and mitigate its evils. Four days hence is the time of its customary approach."

August 25 : " As yet I do not sneeze, nor are my eyes affected. It has not stayed away so long before." August 26 : " Things are *in statu quo*. There is no positive symptom or appearance of catarrh. In driving out yesterday afternoon, the wind freshened up, and I sneezed twice, but John Taylor sneezed three times." Franklin, Aug. 27 : " Thus far the catarrh holds off. It was due the 23rd, but as yet does not show itself." Sept. 8th : " I have been able to keep off the catarrh so far."

Mr. Webster evidently escaped his enemy in the White Mountain region, and narrowly missed the discovery that he escaped it by visiting them. Unfortunately for this discovery, he had fallen into the hands of a friend who appears to have been a sufferer from the June cold, and who advised him to a course of drugs, until, as Mr. Webster says : " My system is so full of iron, potash, and arsenic, that my stomach has become deranged. I took a blue pill last night, and a Rochelle powder this morning. I have had rather a hard time. I have been able to keep off the catarrh so far, but it has called upon me to take so much medicine as a good deal to derange my system. By this process I have lost flesh, and am not a little reduced." Sept. 8 he was free from catarrh, except the eyes, which were " strongly affected, much after the catarrh fashion," in consequence of the heat of the two preceding days. In the afternoon of the 8th, he went to Boston in the railway train. The engine was thrown off the track, and he did not get in before midnight. The next day he was attacked by the catarrh, and it subsequently ran its usual course. Before leaving Boston for Marshfield, he consulted his usual medical adviser, Dr. Jeffries, who promptly discontinued the polypharmacy to which he had been subjected.

Mr. Webster died October 24, 1852, aged seventy, of cirrhosis of the liver and inflammation of the membranes of the brain, without evidence of disease of the lungs or heart. The only peculiarity about the latter organ was an open *foramen ovale*.

CASE 4.

Thomas H. Farnham, Esq., Philadelphia, sends me the following account of his own case : —

I was born in Philadelphia, where I lived during the winter, being in the country during the summer, and returning to the city often before the 20th of August. For eight or ten years past have spent my summers in Beverly, about eighteen miles above Philadelphia, on the opposite side of the river, going to the city daily. Have had catarrh twenty-three years, since I was four years old ; a maternal aunt suffers in the same way, but my parents are both free from it. It commences about the 23d or 24th of August, sometimes perhaps a day or two sooner, with great itching and irritation of the eyes and running thereat ; then sneezing, and running at the nose, which last ten or fifteen days, when it settles on the chest ; the throat is filled with phlegm ; breathing very laborious and difficult, with asthma, for another fortnight, finishing with bronchial irritation, which continues much longer. Never have had asthma at any other time, except once, when I was very much exposed and wet. The asthma is severer at some times than others, particularly after eating heartily ; then it is much worse. When I am suffering from asthma, I am generally free from either running or irritation at the eyes or nose. It lasts till the latter part of September ; by the first of October I am perfectly free from my cold proper ; though sometimes for a year or two past, by not taking proper care of myself when it was passing away, I have had a cough for some time afterwards, generally a slight one, but still annoying. Sensitiveness of the nose and eyes of late years has increased. I am better during and after a cold rain-storm than in dry and dusty weather ; have been in the city sometimes during the whole season, and at various places in the country, with no relief. Was at Cape May one year, and found it aggravated. Never was free from it for the whole season, until 1856, when I was in the highlands of Scotland. I was in England in 1850, in August ; embarked late in that month for New York, where I arrived September 9. I was entirely free until I landed, when the catarrh came on, and lasted till late in the month. For several years was at Andover, Mass., where the disease was somewhat lighter. In 1864 I went to the Glen House with the cold, August 22d, and found entire relief ; went up Mount Washington, and walked down to Crawford's on the 24th ; got wet through ; and while my luggage was coming round, was obliged to dry myself in the sunshine, but without any bad effect.   I stayed at Crawford House and Profile House till September 1st, entirely well. I then went to Andover, Mass., *via* Littleton ; the catarrh came on very badly in the railway train, and I suffered severely all through the month.   In 1865, I arrived at Crawford House August 19th, and during my whole sojourn there, till the 25th September, I did not experience the first symptom of the approach of my annual cold.   I left the Crawford perfectly well upon the morning of the 25th of September, and arrived at Andover, Mass., upon the evening of the following day, without having experienced the slightest annoyance from the long and somewhat dusty ride from Littleton.   I went to Boston upon the day following, and returned in the evening with a slight cold in the head, which I think was induced by the heat and dust of the ride in the " cars," and perhaps, in a greater measure, by my own imprudence in getting somewhat overheated, and afterwards carelessly exposing myself to the air.   I was troubled with a cough, not a very serious or annoying one, however, during October, though I do not think it was any part of my regular annual cold, but was one which I might have taken as easily at another time. Had I remained at the Crawford House until the 1st of October, when the cool weather would have permanently set in, I have not the slightest doubt that I should have had no cold whatever."

Mr. F. had been treated by several different physicians, among them homœopathists, without any other than very temporary relief; and expresses his conviction that there is no other remedy possible, neither prevention nor cure, than change of residence.   " It is my firm and decided belief that any one troubled as we are, has only to remain in the mountains, at least that part of it where I was last summer, for the whole period during which his cold would continue, say from 18th August to 1st October, which I think would cover the whole time, to escape it entirely.   To any one affected like ourselves at that season of that year, I would unhesitatingly recommend the White Mountains, with perfect faith in the efficacy of the remedy."

May 11, 1872, Mr. Farnham writes as follows: " I sailed for Liverpool last summer, August 19th, and had it (in eyes and nose) at the time.   I had not been at sea a day and a half when it entirely disappeared, and I had no return of it whatever.   I returned home October 24th."

CASE 2.   REV. HENRY WARD BEECHER.

BROOKLYN, *September* 25, 1868.

DEAR SIR, — In reply to your request, I will give you some account of the " Hay Fever " to which I am annually subject.

Until I was about thirty-six years of age, I had no symptoms of it. I was not subject to catarrh or colds. On returning from a residence of from twelve to fifteen years in Ohio and Indiana, where I was at various times subject to malarial poison, I settled in Brooklyn, N. Y. The second year of my settlement here, say 1849, while at Woodstock, Ct., I caught cold, as I then supposed, about the middle of August. The next year I noticed that I caught another cold, at just the same time. When, on the same date, the third year, I *caught cold*, I began to inquire about it, and then learned I had *Hay Fever*, or *Hay Asthma*. I have, with the exception of two years, had a return of it so punctual, that I have always admired, rather than desired, this instance of the regularity of nature.

There are four stages of the disease in my case : —

1. From the first of August to the 17th-20th, there is, I am persuaded, a slight febrile disturbance of my system. Ordinarily it is not troublesome, or even noticeable. But, the least cold taken, or the slightest irregularity of diet, developes heat, and a kind of knitting of the sutures of the skull, as if they were slightly moving, or matching themselves over again. Sleep is also full of dreams, not celestial. But the whole passes so lightly, that I did not, until within three years, make it a matter of study.

2. On or about the seventeenth of August, the second stage is developed. My eyes puff out, are very sensitive to light, and full of tears. My nose is exquisitely sensitive, and subject to incessant and copious defluxion. The slightest draft of air produces sneezing of the most enterprising character. To sneeze in tens and twenties, with repeats *ad libitum*, is part of my daily duty. The odor of flowers, smoke and cinders in cars, dust, perfumes, or anything ordinarily without disagreeable effects, n produce sneezing, and a copious secretion of thin and watery mucus. This stage lasts about a week or ten days, — my eyes growing worse, and the light more intolerable. A walk of half an hour in the full sunlight is enough at any time to bring on a paroxysm in every symptom.

3. After about ten days the secretion becomes thicker, the nose is stuffed ; the *eye* grows stronger, but the *lids* are inflamed, and itch incessantly. The *alæ* of the nostrils also are vexed with sharp and itching paroxysms. During all this time my appetite is moderate, digestion good, and sleep undisturbed. Otherwise than the difficulty of using the eyes, there is no hindrance to intellectual labors.

4. About the fourth week the eyes are entirely well, the nose somewhat congested still, but the disease drops down upon the chest, asthma develops, a convulsive cough sets in. In the morning I raise a thick starch-like mucus, without blood, or any other admixture, but like calf's-foot jelly. It has a slightly metallic taste.

This stage lasts about a week or ten days, and then the disease quietly disappears ; or else it breaks up with some row in the system, — such as a breaking out all over the body of itching blotches ; or a violent night of cough and asthma, that wrenches everything about me.

The attack often, in the beginning, comes on so suddenly that whereas at tea I am entirely well, in ten minutes after I am deluged with tears, and flowings at the nose. In other seasons the inception is more gradual.

The same feature is observed in the close. Sometimes it ends so abruptly, that after a night of suffering, I awake without a symptom left. At other times it oozes and creeps away, like a rill gradually drying up.

During the whole period of from five to six weeks, the disease is subject to distinct *remissions*. Although I have had thirty years' experience, I am not cured of believing, every year, that it has ended its career two or three times during its progress. A day of violent perturbation is sure to be followed by a day of quiet. Two or three days of very little disturbance break out into a great uproar. I have not noticed that alternate days are, regularly, well and sick days respectively.

My temperament is mixed, predominantly sanguine nervous, but with a dash of bilious.

As to treatment : After the disease has begun, no treatment has ever checked or cured it. But, where I have taken a preparatory course, I have sensibly alleviated it, and shortened its term.

It should be added, that I live during July, August, and September, at Peekskill, forty miles above New York, on the Hudson River, among the highlands, on a high, dry, and warm piece of land. I have never spen .. summer in the city, and shall never, if I can help myself. I had rather have " Hay Fever."

The two summers that I visited Europe, I was entirely free from it. During the week that it was due (in 1863) I was in the Tyrol. On the seventeenth of August it came, knocked, and looked in upon me, but did not stop. There was a single hour of mild but unmistakable symptoms, and only one.

I have abundant evidence that change, not of place, but of climate, will prevent it. The Catskill Mountain House is filled every summer with fugitives from " Hay Fever," and they find immunity. Some of my friends escape it by going to the Adirondacs, and some by a tour through the Lake Superior region. The Fire Island Hotel is a great resort of New Yorkers who are afflicted with ophthalmic catarrh. Fire Island is about fifty miles from New York, on the ocean coast of Long Island.

A sister is a sufferer, and a brother's son. No others of our

family have been attacked.   Many gentlemen in New York arrange
their business so as to make an August voyage to Europe, thus escaping the inception. .

A lady sends me word that she has cured herself permanently by
using sulphur three times a day, as we used to take it when children.

If there are any other points on which I can give you further
information, I shall be happy to do so.   .

I am very truly yours,
HENRY WARD BEECHER.

MORRILL WYMAN, M. D., *Cambridge, Mass.*

In 1871 Mr. Beecher was completely relieved at Twin
Mountain House, White Mountain region.

CASE 1. HENRY W. HAYNES, Esq.

35 COURT STREET, BOSTON, *October* 26, 1860.

DR. MORRILL WYMAN,

Dear Sir, — Understanding that you are desirous of receiving a
written statement of the characteristics of my " case " of " *Hay
Fever,*" I hasten to transmit it, sincerely hoping that your studies
may result in some discovery beneficial to all of us companions in
misfortune.

I was born in Bangor, Me., and lived there till my tenth year,
when we removed to Boston, where I lived till the summer of 1846,
when we removed to Cambridge in my fifteenth year.   My trouble
commenced that autumn (which I recollect as very hot, dry, and
dusty), and has continued till the present time, varying in intensity.
This year it began somewhat later than usual, upon August 26th, instead of August 20th, when it usually commences.   I went to bed
perfectly well ; in the night the wind changed to the west, and when
I woke my nose began to run.   From that day till now I have remained in Boston all the time, and have not suffered very much,
though the complaint has lingered longer than usual, and has entirely disappeared only within a few days.

In three different years I have suffered from difficulty of breathing, which has been entirely relieved by the use of French medicated
cigarettes.   I find my complaint much aggravated by hot, dry, and
dusty weather, and riding in the cars at such times makes me very
unwell indeed ; while in damp, rainy, or cold weather, and in east
winds, I am a great deal better.

Two years ago I was troubled very much in Boston, and went
down to the Isles of Shoals, where I arrived much worse from the
journey.   I do not think I derived any benefit from the air there ;
certainly I suffered more from difficulty of breathing than ever
before.

A year ago I went to the White Mountains, intending to be there at the time when the trouble began, and to remain there some time. I escaped with merely the slightest symptoms of a cold in the head, and was perfectly well for several days after the ordinary period of attack. Business, however, compelled me to return to town earlier than I had anticipated. I left the Profile House early in the morning perfectly well, and was perfectly well when I entered the cars at Plymouth, but after riding an hour my trouble commenced, and it had its regular career that year, accompanied with difficulty of breathing.

In 1855 I was in Europe, and left Paris for Switzerland at about the period of attack. After riding all day in the diligence from Dole to Geneva, over a dry, dusty, limestone country, on arriving at Geneva, I was in a bad condition. But all the next day I remained in my hotel, taking laxative medicines, and on the following morning started for Chamouny ; my trouble left me forthwith, and I suffered no more that year.

Sometimes the disease is accompanied by great inflammation of the eyes, but for the last two years this symptom has not appeared.

My attacks begin August 20th (or within a day or two of that date) by a slight stuffing up of the nose — by a week I begin to sneeze — paroxysms principally in the morning on first getting up, so that sometimes it takes me more than an hour to get into a condition to permit of my attempting to eat; also I am subject to paroxysms in the evening, apparently caused by night air ; and sometimes at other times in the day; by a fortnight my eyes are greatly inflamed and my throat very sore; these symptoms continue about a fortnight without much abatement, then the bronchial tubes and lungs begin to be affected, and the symptoms in the head grow less severe ; sometimes I have an asthmatic attack, but by no means every year; The running from the nose lasts up to the very end of the attack, which is at the beginning of cool (or rather coldish) weather, say the first slight frost ; but this running is most severe about the middle of the disease.

I have never noticed any effect produced by exercise, but I always find great relief in damp and rainy weather ; the hotter and dryer the season the greater are my sufferings. It seemed to me (up to last season) that my attacks were growing less severe year by year, but last year I had the worst time of any, and was perfectly prostrated by the complaint, and did not get over it till December. I have never experienced any relief from medicines and medical treatment, though I have tried a great many remedies which others have said to be efficacious in their own cases.

I am much better in the city than in the country. In 1864 I was in London during the period of the attack, and entirely escaped, not perceiving the slightest symptom, but having returned home on October 1st, I was slightly affected after that time only in the nose. However, this exemption, as also when I escaped attack by being in Switzerland in 1855, was followed by a severer attack in the following year. The sea-side only benefits me by its being cooler there, but the mountain air seems to afford me a remedy. I have not been at the White Mountains since 1860, and I have never noticed any difference in the effect of one side of the range from that of the other.

To sum up my own experience of what procured me the most freedom and relief from suffering, I keep in the city as much as possible, avoiding going into the country, and particularly riding in the cars, as their dust and smoke is the most exciting cause of the stuffing up and sneezing that I know. I keep in the shade, as sunlight makes me sneeze; I live lightly, and avoid wine and liquors; don't eat much meat; keep as cool as possible, especially at night; and then if the season is decently cool, and there is no drought, I get along pretty well. I think my eyes have not troubled me so much of late years as they did before I understood better how to manage myself.

I find that the scent of full-blown roses makes me sneeze, and once I was picking strawberries in a hay-field in July, and suddenly found myself attacked by a violent fit of sneezing and running of the eyes; but it soon left me after I had bathed my head in cold water, and retired to a cool room.

I wish that I felt a little more able to "deliver" a more "varnished tale," but I believe I have stated everything that occurs to me as likely to be of service to you. I ought to state that I think the "cold" is a disease, attacking the whole system, and attended with a good deal of fever; certainly it often makes me very sick, used up, and good for nothing; but on the other hand, I never suffer from colds, or very rarely, and enjoy good health, having never been sick before this malarial fever, caught on the bar of the Mississippi River.

I suppose you ought to know that my father was a great sufferer from asthma, when I was born, and died at the age of thirty-seven, of consumption; my mother is living, and is perfectly healthy.

It is needless to state that I have tried numerous remedies without success, and that I have no confidence in any alleviation except the air of the mountains; if I cannot be there, I think I suffer less in the city.

Hoping that your studies may prove beneficial as well in your own case as in that of others, I am, . Very truly yours,

HENRY W. HAYNES.

CASE 60.

For the following case I am indebted to Dr. George Derby, of Boston : —

Mrs. G. D., Boston, has had catarrh since ten years of age, which she remembers to have first noticed when peaches were ripe, a basket of them immediately producing catarrhal symptoms in the nose and eyes ; so would certain flowers, the geranium, and especially the heliotrope, but not the rose. An annual catarrh has for the past six or eight years commenced between the 15th and 18th of August, and continued till about the 1st of October, or until frost. The first indications are itching and watering of the eyes ; the itching is almost intolerable, especially at the inner angles of the eyes ; profuse discharge of limpid water from the nostrils, especially in the afternoon. In a day or two there is itching in the back part of the throat, and near the upper part of the larynx, and in the roof of the mouth. The nostrils are very seldom obstructed as in an ordinary cold. In the night, if the windows are carefully closed, she has but little trouble, but if they are open, she suffers more than during the day. The senses of taste and of smell are impaired. This state of things continues about two weeks, when irritation commences in the throat, with cough, at first slight and not very frequent, and without expectoration. This cough increases, and during the last two weeks becomes extremely annoying, and almost incessant while lying down, compelling her to sleep in an almost upright position. The disease may be considered as at its height on 1st September. From this time all the troubles diminish ; the head symptoms first, the discharge from the nostrils becoming gradually less profuse and more consistent, and the cough less constant and irritating, and by the first of October the disease has disappeared. The influence upon the system generally exhibits itself in a loss of strength, loss of appetite and flesh, also a sense of chilliness of the whole body, which prompts her to use more clothing than most persons, especially at night. She is never so comfortable as when so warmly covered as to produce more or less perspiration. She thinks the disease has increased in severity during the past few years. As a girl she had no cough. For several years resided in Cambridge, and suffered much while there. If she went to Boston, and walked in the hot sun, she would be almost entirely free, but would experience a renewal of the paroxysms on her return to Cambridge. During several seasons she was at Swampscot, Nahant, or Newport, all of them at the sea-side, without any relief. In 1862, '63, and '64, went to the White Mountains. In 1862, she was suffering severely in Cambridge, and went to the White Mountain Notch (Crawford House), and remained ten weeks with complete relief. She then returned to Cambridge, and suffered two weeks longer severely; in fact, she suffered till the end of the usual period. In 1863 she got no relief at North Conway, about twenty miles south of the White Mountains, and went to the Crawford House again, where she was relieved, but not entirely. She then went to the Profile House, at Franconia, and during the ride over improved; on her arrival was nearly well, and remained entirely free from her enemy during that year, returning home October 1st. She never suffered from asthmatic breathing until September, 1864, four months previous to the birth of her first child. She then suffered severely, and went to Franconia for relief. She was much annoyed during the railway ride by the cough and asthma. The air was cold and damp, without sufficient fires, at Franconia, and although she tried various remedies, she got no relief, during the whole season suffering as much in every respect as ever before. 1865 she passed in Augusta, Maine. The attack came on at the usual time, and she suffered as severely as at Cambridge; going into the garden, or into the dusty street, brought on a paroxysm of sneezing, itching of the eyes and ears, and the other usual head symptoms.

As far as medical treatment goes, she has not taken much. Morphine has not given her so much relief as the "elixir of opium," which diminishes all the head symptoms, but as it produces nausea, she has used it but little. The snuffing of Cologne water, or strong alcohol, gives relief. She has tried the burning of paper impregnated with saltpetre, and she smoked the arsenical cigarettes during the year she had asthma, without relief. In fact, nothing has given her relief but a residence at the White Mountains during the period of attack.

In 1868, Mrs. D. was at the Waumbec House, Jefferson Hill, but after a week's residence there without relief, returned home by the way of Littleton and Plymouth. "I suffered there from our horrid cold as much as I ever did in Cambridge. I was sorely disappointed, for I had persuaded my husband to take us up there, promising him that I should be well, and should have no use for a handkerchief, and should breathe like an infant, if I could only be on Jefferson Hill. Such is life.

"The ride in the cars was terrible torture to me; cinders poison me more than flames. I really thought I should choke to death. The asthmatic part of the affection increases with my years. I cannot sleep like a Christian."

CASE 57.

The following case was sent me by my friend, the late Dr. Anson Hooker, of East Cambridge, Mass. : —

Mrs. A. H., when eighteen, first noticed being affected by the aroma of roses. The following year, while picking some roses, felt an itching in her eyes. This was in the morning. The itching increased, and by afternoon was so intolerable, she asked medical advice. After this she could not be in a room where there were bouquets, or many flowers, without itching of the eyes and other catarrhal symptoms; often obliged to leave an omnibus when large bouquets were present. This state of things continued for about ten years, when she began to have the regular Autumnal Catarrh. After this she was not so sensitive to the aroma of flowers; still she could not be much in their immediate atmosphere and not feel their influence. We can never have many flowers in the house unless in a glass vase. This much I premise before speaking of her Autumnal Catarrh.

She must have been about twenty-eight years of age when she began to have her periodical attacks, or to notice them as periodical. At this time she resided at East Cambridge, and since; in fact, her residence has been here since she was fourteen years of age.

She has tried change of residence during the attacks. She first tried Nantucket;[1] was more comfortable while in the town of Nantucket proper, but not very decidedly relieved. The air at Siasconset, a little village at the opposite end of the island, was too bracing or irritating to the mucous surfaces already inflamed. How it might have been if she had gone there before the catarrhal attack came on, is a question. She has also tried the Isles of Shoals. While there, she has had the attacks milder, but not so great freedom from them as to counterbalance the discomforts of being from home. At Mount Holyoke she is pretty comfortable till the winds blow hard, and fogs come upon the mountain; then she starts for home.

The severity of the attacks vary with the seasons and her exposure. If, while the attack is on her, she is much exposed to dust, as in travelling, or to be out in a breezy day, or to be obliged to talk very much, the troubles are much aggravated. She is not aware that under the usual circumstances the attacks are more severe of late years than formerly. Indeed, I think she suffers rather less than formerly, because we *prepare* and *protect* her better than we used to.

The attack comes regularly during the third week in August.

The eyes are the first to be affected, then the nose, throat, the ears, and bronchia. The itching of the eyes and nose and throat is intolerable, and very much aggravated by rubbing, blowing of the nose, or talking, or singing, or much exercise. There is a profuse

---

[1] Nantucket is an island lying off the southern coast of Massachusetts, about twenty-five miles from the main-land. The Isles of Shoals are a group of small islands, eight or ten miles distant from Portsmouth, N. H.

watery secretion from the nostrils, and considerable mucous discharge from the throat and lungs. At times has asthmatic attacks — the feeling of breathing through gauze or sponge. She has had so much of this catarrhal inflammation, that the mucous membrane of the nostrils is permanently thickened, obstructing them to such an extent as to oblige her to sleep with her mouth open. The cough and mucous expectoration does not come on till the attack has existed a fortnight or more.

Is better in quiet, dry weather; is worse in damp, windy, dusty weather. Heat or cold does not disturb. No itching of the skin. Is now fifty-two.

She thinks she is as comfortable in her own quiet chamber as anywhere. In windy days, to shut up tight, and keep as far as possible all vexatious intruders away. Cannot be out in the damp evenings of September. The first *good* frost in October is a godsend to her; till that comes, her troubles last, and she is not even relieved.

Our aim is to put her in the best state of health we can before the season of the attack, that she may the better bear the misery that awaits her. If she is otherwise in good health, I think the attacks are less severe.

Inhaling moderately chloroform has relieved the nostrils more than anything. Of course the effect is but temporary.

I will add, that all fruits in an uncooked state, except strawberries, inflame the mouth and throat, and bring on itching. Melons, tomatoes, etc., sliced and placed upon the table, have to be removed. If she pares an apple or an orange, the eyes and nose are immediately in trouble, and this at any season of the year.

Mrs. B., her elder sister, has some of the same affections, but not so persistently. Her attacks are occasional. Itching of the eyes and difficulty of breathing are her principal annoyances.

DEAR DR. WYMAN, — The above, I believe, answers all your inquiries about Mrs. H.'s catarrhal history, which I am very happy to give you. If yours is any worse, *we* pity you; if it is not so bad, we know what you must suffer.

Some of our acquaintances have been benefited by living at Fire Island, off New York, where Margaret Fuller was shipwrecked.

Sincerely yours, etc.,

July 20th, 1865.   ANSON HOOKER.

CASE 7.

For the following account of his own case, I am indebted to the late John C. Hayden, M. D., of Cambridge, Mass: —

BOSTON, *October* 19, 1857.

DEAR DOCTOR, — My reason for not answering immediately your inquiries respecting my annual catarrh, was that I had not any dates or notes as to its progress and symptoms, to which I could refer. I believe, however, that I can give you all the information you desire from memory alone, which has just been so perfectly refreshed as to the symptoms. During a period of at least thirty years, I have had an annual return of this affection about the last week in August; its commencement, symptoms, and progress, have always been about the same. It always commences with a heaviness of the eyelids, itching of the inner canthi, and occasional sneezing. After a few days there comes on an inflammation of the mucous membrane of the nostrils, extending upward to the frontal sinuses and eyelids, and downward to the velum palati, pouring forth a profuse thin secretion; frequent and protracted sneezing, sense of tightness in the forehead; a spasmodic closing of the nasal passages, suddenly relieved by a change to a warmer or colder atmosphere, and as suddenly recurring, without apparent cause. The same spasm occasionally extends to the bronchi, producing slight asthma, neuralgic pains about the head, and in various parts of the body, lassitude, depression of spirits, burning sensation extending down the œsophagus to the stomach; the digestive organs are not affected. No cough, excepting sufficient to dislodge a somewhat increased secretion from the lungs. These symptoms continue about three weeks, and then abate gradually, until the 1st of October, when they disappear entirely.

I suffer less from the disease than in former years, and find that it commences later; it is much less severe in the city than in the country, and is much aggravated by exposure to night air. The only remedies I have used have been external applications to the eyes and head, and inhalations of the vapor of hot water, ether, alcohol, etc., but I have received from them but slight relief. I have given you above as full a description as I am able of my September cold; and if it assists you in your investigations of the disease, it will much gratify,   Yours sincerely,

J. C. HAYDEN.

Dr. Hayden's health was generally good, until his death by apoplexy in 1869.

CASE 28.

For the following case — that of the Hon. Lemuel Shaw, late Chief Justice of the Supreme Court of Massachusetts — I am indebted to his son, Lemuel Shaw, Esq., of Boston; and also to the late Dr. George Hayward, of Boston : —

He had suffered from youth with annually returning attacks of catarrh, which commenced between the 20th and 22d of August (or, as Dr. Hayward thinks, August 18th, almost at the same hour of the day). It was ushered in by pretty strong febrile symptoms, — pain in the head, rapid pulse, a hot and dry skin. After one or two days appeared the unmistakable catarrhal symptoms, especially a severe cough, with a very copious discharge of viscid mucus. When near the end of the first stage he had attacks of asthma, generally each night ; but more certainly, and with more severity after active movements, ascending a hill, mounting stairs, or after a rich meal. He was probably more liable to these attacks after exertion, on account of his weight, which was considerably above that of most persons (more than two hundred pounds). After about five weeks came the last stage, during which Judge Shaw was obliged to make a railway journey of some forty miles, to hold court. The disease did not disappear before the middle of October ; a stay, therefore, of about seven weeks. One year he left Liverpool September 20th, and arrived in Boston October 1st. He was perfectly well until his arrival in Boston ; but within two days the disease appeared, and went through its regular course.

His last access, in 1860, at the age of eighty, was less severe than the preceding ; but almost from the commencement appeared signs of organic disease of the heart, which was developed after the catarrh had passed, but not sufficiently for special diagnosis ; the movements of the heart were increased and violent. There was water in the pericardium, thorax, abdomen, and under the skin. Still the general health remained tolerably good. He was able to ride in the open air, or walk ; and even the second day before his death he could attend to his professional duties. Finally, in March, 1861, brain symptoms appeared ; he was restless, incoherent in his speech, had hallucinations, with short periods of deep sleep, followed by a speedy and quick death from effusion upon the brain. There was no examination *post mortem*.

Doctor Hayward was of opinion that the heart disease was increased, if not produced, by the breast symptoms of the catarrh, especially by the long continued obstruction of the circulation through the lungs.

The mother of Judge Shaw had Autumnal Catarrh, and he was the only child who arrived at maturity. Judge S. had four children. One son has Autumnal Catarrh ; one son and one daughter have summer catarrh in June. The son who has Autumnal Catarrh has a daughter, now twenty-two years of age, who for six or eight years has had Autumnal Catarrh; a son has neither of the diseases, although arrived at adult age.

CASES 5 AND 6.

To Dr. George H. Lyman, of Boston, Mass., I am indebted for the following history of cases : —

BOSTON, *May* 26, 1866.

MY DEAR DOCTOR WYMAN, — I hasten to answer your note as to Autumnal Catarrh. I am only sorry that I shall be able to give you so little that will be satisfactory. The only two cases which I have had under observation from the *very inception* of the disease, and continuing under observation for any length of time, namely, eight or ten years, or more, were my own son, and the son of Amos A. Lawrence, Esq. I give in brief the details, so far as my memory serves me ; for such notes as I had have been lost or displaced during my five years in the army.

My son, now fifteen years of age, when two or three years old, was attacked in August; duration until cold weather; most severe last of August, beginning with snuffling, and soon profuse discharge from Schneiderian membrane, and, almost simultaneously, itching, congestion, and lachrymation ; deglutition somewhat interfered with, though no marked trouble of ears or throat ; cough never severe, and more due apparently to the irritating nasal secretion than to any positive affection of the posterior air passages. Asthma slight, and no appreciable pulmonary symptoms; general health, strength, and flesh but slightly affected. Smoke, night air (especially about sunset), and gaslight, always aggravating the oppression and discharge. As year after year its periodicity became more certain, different summer localities were selected : under Blue Hill, at Milton ; Nahant, Swampscot, Springfield, and town residence ; and last year the White Mountains. No apparent difference, though for the last few years the intensity of the attacks has gradually diminished. Last year, at Conway, was quite as bad as the year before at Swampscot. I *think* there has always been some irritability of the skin during the attacks. The congestion and secretion from eyes and nose are always present ; but paroxysmal aggravations of short duration coming on at intervals of an hour or two, more or less.

I have exhausted the Materia Medica upon him, — iodine, potash (separately or combined), arsenic, opiates, expectorants, etc., — but without any appreciable benefit. I have at last concluded that strict attention to the digestive organs has been of more service than all the rest. *He* thinks that a dose of Tully's powder (Dover's powder and camphor) at night has given him relief, and I think he is

right. He is now, and has been, away for a year at school, in
Concord, N. H., except in summer vacation ; and thought that the
duration of the disease, on his return thither in September, was
much shortened.

The other case — that of young L. — commenced at Lynn, in
September, 1852, he being, I think, four years old. The attack was
very sudden and severe, alarmingly so. I supposed it a case of
bronchitis; it lasted, however, a long time. The febrile symptoms
soon yielded, but the irritation of the mucous membrane was not
allayed until cold weather, and was early accompanied by severe
asthmatic paroxysms, the eyes and nose being affected as in ordinary severe catarrh. I think there was no trouble about the ears,
throat, or skin. I think in October he was removed to Concord,
Mass., and there remained some weeks. I should say that the face
became puffy and swollen from the severity of the asthmatic com-
plication. These attacks recurred annually about the same period,
but never again accompanied by the severe pulmonary symptoms.
He is now strong and hearty, and I think has about, if not quite,
outgrown the difficulty. I have never been able to satisfy myself
that he was benefited by remedies ; but Mr. L.'s house, at Lynn,
directly on the sea, was always unfavorable to him, and inland localities less so.

I shall look with interest for your published views ; and if you
can enlighten us, you will have the satisfaction of removing one of
the opprobria of the art or science.

I am, my dear doctor, most respectfully and sincerely yours,
GEORGE H. LYMAN.

July 18, 1871, Doctor Lyman informs me that his son
has been somewhat relieved by the use of sulphate of quinine, which he directs from the middle of July in doses of
two grains twice daily. But he has received the greatest
relief by a visit to the White Mountains, at Gorham, and
at Success, a town six or eight miles further north. In the
latter town he was in camp, at a distance from cultivation
of all kinds, and was quite well.

CASE 3.

For the following description of his own case I am indebted to John J. Dixwell, Esq., of Boston, Mass : —

I have suffered from Autumnal Catarrh since forty-five years of age,
about fifteen years. The attack begins between the 25th and 28th of

August, with paroxysms of sneezing and affection of the eyes. The affection of the eyes one year preceded by three weeks the other decided symptoms of catarrh, the eyelids becoming glutinous and uncomfortable. I have never suffered from itching of the internal ear nor of the soft palate. Early in September a bronchial affection sets in, when the nasal catarrh has diminished, and continues through the month and sometimes through the whole winter. I have never had asthmatic troubles, although I have had some difficulty of breathing in going up hill, which has increased very much during the last two or three years, caused by a certain degree of enlargement of the heart. During the attacks I lose flesh and strength. The severity of the whole disease varies somewhat in different seasons; the time of commencement of the attack depends somewhat upon accidental exciting causes; a ride in the railway train with its smoke and dust, or a visit to a cotton mill will hasten the period of annual attack materially.

My first attack was while living in Boston and vicinity, mostly in Boston, and I perceived no difference in severity whether I was in Boston or the country. One year I spent entirely in Boston, except in the afternoon, but without relief. It gradually increased in severity at each annual return, and I found myself now liable to catarrhal affections at other seasons of the year. But I have never had the June or "Rose Cold," or any catarrhal affection before the 25th of August.

Each year since 1863 I have visited one or more of the various places of summer resort in the White Mountains, Gorham, the Glen House at the foot of Mt. Washington, the Crawford House, and the Waumbec House in Jefferson, and during these three years I have had no attack of catarrh, although I have had some slight irritation, not enough to annoy me; no irritation of the eyes or throat, no cough. I arrive at the mountains from August 22d to August 24th. In no other place have I been relieved; the sea-coast aggravates my troubles. One year I went from Gorham down to North Conway (twenty miles south on a lower level and in a valley); I remained there two days and a half, but was obliged to return to the mountains; the catarrh attacked me and steadily increased; I then went to Crawford's, and was free from it for the rest of the season. The general tendency to catarrh at other seasons, which was previously increasing, has greatly diminished since my first visit to Gorham, in 1863.

I have tried a great variety of remedies — balsam of copaiba, until its peculiar eruption was produced; nux vomica, strychnine, cubebs, inhaling the smoke of burning powdered opium; I have derived the most relief from morphine; laudanum and glycerine applied to the nostrils has given relief.

A brother of Mr. D. is also subject to the disease; his first attack was much later in life.

JEFFERSON, *September* 25, 1868.

MY DEAR SIR, — I cannot answer your note better than by giving you my own experience : —

My cold did not formerly come on till the 27th or 28th of August, but a railroad ride of some hours has always precipitated it temporarily, when coming up here some days earlier, and I have more of it in dry and hot weather than in cool and damp days. For the two years past my case has been modified by some enlargement of the heart. Asthma with shortness of breath, has prevented exercise, and impaired my former vigor.

Last year I left on the 24th, for Burlington, Vt., going through in a day, and wearing a veil. It had rained the day before between Boston and Rutland, but at Burlington they were parched up by a long drought. I got the cold about twenty miles from Boston, had it all day, and had a dreadful night at Burlington. It lingered about me at times there, and on the way to Stow for two days. On the 27th, I went to the top of Mt. Mansfield, and found myself entirely relieved; came down to Stow next day, and remained there well two days. I found there Commodore I. of Philadelphia, who has suffered for fifteen years, and who was then nine days over his time, at Stow, without any cold. I then went on to Jefferson, suffered again on the cars, and had another bad night at Littleton, though not so bad as before. Reached Jefferson on the 3d, and remained there till the 26th of September. For several days after my arrival, I had occasional attacks of catarrh, and my eyes were considerably inflamed, and through the whole month I had more of it than ever before at the mountains. Still my condition was vastly better than it had ever been in Boston during the same period, and comparatively I might call it relief.

This year I left home a good deal fagged, on the 22d, after a copious rain which had laid the dust all through the country. I had some catarrh before I left home, and took a small dose of morphine before breakfast, and it increased through the day. I wore a veil, but my eyes became very much inflamed, and I reached Willoughby Lake at 7 P. M. and had a pretty good night. I remained there almost free from catarrh, but with my eyes considerably inflamed, till the 29th, when it came on. The air was very much loaded with smoke from burning woods. On the 30th and 31st, I was on my way *via* Island Pond, to Gorham, riding through a district full of smoke; arrived at Gorham 31st at 9½ A. M. and went on to Jefferson on the morning of September 1st, with the cold all the way till we were four or five miles from Gorham, when we had a copious rain of an hour, washing the atmosphere, and bringing much relief at once. It took several days to allay the irritation of my eyes, and I have had some slight and short inconvenience at times, but the relief here may be said to be almost complete, and my general condition greatly invigorated.

There were some sixteen or eighteen persons here last year, and about as many this, all enjoying entire, or very nearly entire relief; the exceptions being only short and temporary; among them Mr. and Mrs. W., of Boston, who are both curious and severe cases. He was perfectly well for the first time in twelve, and Mrs. W. (with the exception of a single day after unusual exposure) for the first time in twenty-four years.

I infer that my experiments in moving about to try new places, and my own impaired condition, have exposed me more during the last two years, and thus account for the less favorable result on myself, especially as others do not appear to have been similarly affected, and consider that the air here may be regarded as sure to give an amount of relief almost, if not quite complete.

Very truly yours,
J. J. DIXWELL.

CASE 9.

Mr. Fisk, the writer of the following letters, was born in Cambridge, Mass., and suffered from Autumnal Catarrh before he was twelve years old. At sixteen he had an affection of the lungs, for which he went to Cuba. While in college at New Haven, Conn., and also when in Boston, Mass., he had his annual attacks; but during several autumns spent at Saratoga he had some relief. In 1857 he removed from Cambridge to St. Paul, Minnesota, on the Mississippi, and from that city sent me the following letters : —

ST. PAUL, MINN., September 14, 1857.

In a letter recently received, I learned that you were making inquiries about the condition of my head, eyes, lungs, etc., at this time, and whether I was escaping any of the annoying symptoms of the catarrh which have heretofore so much affected me at this season of the year. As I have heretofore been more severely affected than any one I ever knew who is troubled in a like manner, I did not expect wholly to escape this year. Usually I have been taken about the 20th of August, as with a slight cold in the head. You know the progress of the complaint very well; about this time and for a week before I usually have had a high fever every afternoon, and after nightfall have had great difficulty in breathing.   By the 25th of September I have generally been pretty well again, excepting my eyes have been rather weak, and the mucous membrane of the air passages generally a little sensitive.   During this summer I have not had that dryness of the fauces and the nostrils which has formerly been the case.   As the 20th of August approached, I watched for the early stage of the catarrh to appear, but was so free from any affection of that kind, that on the 25th I rode out some three or four hours ride into the country through corn, wheat, rye, and oat fields, without any inconvenience, and returned the next day in the same manner.   Up to the present time I have been free from any of the symptoms of the catarrh, excepting perhaps one or two mornings, when I felt as if I had taken cold slightly, during the night, which is not at all improbable, as the head of my bed stands close to the open window, and the wind was blowing directly on to me all night.   I have been thus particular, as you expressed a desire to know how I was passing through this period of the year, and I have escaped so well; the result would probably be the same with any other, which is the fact you wish to get at.

We have a most beautiful country, not surpassed in the whole West.   The great charm is in the climate.   We are at an elevation of about eight hundred feet above the level of the sea.   We have a dry, bracing, exhilarating, invigorating, and pure atmosphere.   This climate is peculiarly favorable to persons having any pulmonary weakness.   There are persons in this town, in the enjoyment of good health, who would have been in their graves long since, had they not come to this territory.   If a person is heard coughing in this city, we know, without asking, that he or she, as the case may be, "has just come up the river."   Coughs and colds are exotics in this climate.

STATE LIBRARY, ST. PAUL, MINN., September 12, 1862.

My autumn cold, when I lived at the east, was very punctual in its advent about the 20th of August.   The mucous membrane of all the air passages in time became very much inflamed.   For many nights after the 1st of September, till about the 12th, I was unable to get any comfortable sleep, because of the severe attacks of asthma, which were always a part of the infliction, and generally every afternoon I was mentally and physically prostrated by a hot, dry, burning fever.

Since I have been in St. Paul, I have known nothing about an autumn cold, such as I knew it at the east.   At the east I suffered severely from inflammation of the eyes, which inflammation extended all through that region of the head.   I have had nothing of the kind here.   At the east, usually for one full month, I was unfit for any duty, but now I am able to accomplish a full day's work every day from the 1st of August till the 1st of October.

In my judgment, a person coming from the east here, merely to avoid having the cold at the usual time, would not wholly escape. I was east during the summer of 1859, and on my return reached home about 20th August. I brought back with me enough of the eastern influence to give me some trouble for two or three weeks.

I think I received more relief from the use of iodide of potassium, with the syrup of sarsaparilla, than from any other medicine I ever used.   Very truly yours,

ROBERT F. FISK.

Mr. F. suffered much during his attacks from the irritability of the mouth, tonsils, and fauces, which became red and sensitive during the progress of the disease. He remained in Minnesota till 1863. From June till October of that year he suffered from what was supposed to be rheumatism, a painful affection of the feet, ankles, and legs, compelling him to keep his bed most of the time. In December he had so far recovered as to make the journey to Washington, although he had a severe cough. Soon after his arrival in Washington, while walking in the street, he was seized with difficult breathing, and died in about fifteen minutes, at the age of forty-four.

CASE 58.

Mrs. J. B., age 46. Since sixteen years old had a cold in *June* most severe when hay was in the field; first felt when in New Bedford, Mass., while walking in a garden. It commenced with sneezing, watering and itching of the eyes, itching of the back of the throat, and in the ears, also itching of the whole scalp. The discharge of limpid water from the nostrils was most profuse, saturating a handkerchief in a few minutes. During damp weather, much less trouble, some days none; dry, dusty weather increased it, but heat had little or no influence. The first *Autumnal Catarrh* was about 1st of September, 1850, at Fitchburg, Mass., while on the way home from the White Mountains. From that time to this, the attacks have recurred annually. While the June Cold has very much diminished in severity and in length, still she is even now annoyed by going into a hay-field, or even into a barn when the hay is moved, even in winter, or by dusty carpets. All these causes produce sneezing, watering of the eyes, and tickling of the throat. The early symptoms of the Autumnal Catarrh are almost precisely like those of the June Cold. It commences about the 17th of August, and increases till the 1st of

September, at which time a cough commences, which she never had with the June Cold, and which now is not severe. From the 1st of September the head symptoms begin to diminish, varying with the season, and especially with the dryness of the weather, which invariably increases its severity and prolongs its duration. The irritation of the skin, especially of the scalp, is quite annoying, and the irritation of the nostrils and the sneezing are more severe on first rising in the morning, and while dressing the hair. During the disease, her strength is reduced, and her appetite and flesh decidedly lessened. The natural termination of her troubles is the 1st of October.

She tried a residence at various places, but usually at Belmont, Mass. During three seasons she was at sea in August and September, and escaped the autumn cold entirely. She also escaped the June Cold during the four years she was in England, or on the Continent, and suffered less from it in Boston. For the autumnal cold she has never tried the sea-coast. She arrived at the White Mountains in the train on Saturday, September 1st, with a very severe attack. The following day she was better, and on Monday well, and so remained during the ten days she was there. On her return to Belmont, she again experienced some trouble, but by no means severe. For the past two years she has resided in Boston, but has had no relief from her autumn cold. Nux vomica, and a great variety of medicines, have given no relief. Cubebs have relieved her somewhat, and the irritation of the nostrils has been lessened by cayenne pepper and ammonia.

Mrs. B. went to New Brunswick, Maine, August 7, 1866, then to Bangor, and remained well till September 5. On that day, took the evening train for the White Mountains; reached Jefferson Hill the same day, and remained well till October 1st. She then returned to Belmont, and in a few days went to Philadelphia. Immediately on her arrival in Philadelphia, she was seized with the usual symptoms of Autumnal Catarrh, which did not abate until she went to New York a week afterwards. The flowers were in full bloom in Philadelphia during her visit there.

No.	Name.	Age.	Age when First Attacked.	Profession or Occupation.	ANNUAL ATTACK. Beginning.	ANNUAL ATTACK. End.	Head Symptoms.	Chest Symptom Cough.	Chest Symptom Asth
1	H. W. H.	30	15	Lawyer	August 20	October 1	3	2	
2	H. W. B.	58	36	Clergyman . . .	About August 17 .	About October 1	3	3	
3	J. J. D.	60	45	President of Bank	August 11-15 . . .	October 1	2	2	
4	T. H. F.	27	4	Merchant . . .	August 23, 24 . . .	October 1	3	2	
5	G. L.	15	3 or 4	Student	August	Cold weather	3	1	1
6	L.	16	4	Student	September 1 . . .	October	1	–	
7	J. C. H.	57	27	Physician . . .	Last week in Aug.	October 1	3	–	
8	D. W.	70	50	Statesman . . .	August 23	Last week in Sept. or first week in Oct.	3	2	
9	R. F. F.	35	12	Merchant . . .	August 20	September 25	3	3	
10	M. W.	55	21	Physician . . .	August 23, 24 . . .	October 1	3	3	
11	E. F. A.	15	10	Student	August 20	September 25-30	3	2	
12	W. P. A.	51	18	Manufacturer . .	August 15	First frost	2	2	
13	N. M. H.	42	23	Manufacturer . .	August 20	October 1	2	2	
14	M. W. Jr.	15	11	Student	August 24	October 1	3	2	
15	E. W.	49	25	Merchant . . .	August 15-24 . . .	Third week in September	3	1	
16	A. E. N.	36	24	Manufacturer . .	Last week in Aug.	First or second week in October . .	1	3	
17	J. K. F.	49	46	Gardener . . .	Third week in Aug.	Cold weather	3	3	
18	G. C. W.	43	6 or 7	Farmer . . .	August 20-23 . .	First hard frost	3	1	
19	C. P. H.	36	10	Carpenter . . .	August 15 . . .	Frosty nights	3	2	
20	W. H. Y. H.	66	31	Lawyer	August 16-25 . .	First black frost	3	3	
21	W. P. J.	55	20	Merchant . . .	Aug. 20-Sept. 5 . .	In four weeks	3	0	
22	S. R.	87	24	Manufacturer . .	August 24-31 . . .	Frosty weather	3	3	
23	E. S. D.	63	46	Teacher	August 15-20 . .	September 25	3	3	
24	J. H.	68	31	Manufacturer . .	August 20	First frost	3	3	
25	H. A. R.	50	30	Merchant . . .	August 20	September 25	3	3	
26	J. P.	46	45	Merchant . . .	August 23	September 20-30	3	2	
27	F. P.	25	8 or 10	Farmer . . .	August 19	October 1	3	3	
28	L. S.	80	From youth	Jurist	August 18	First or second week in October . .	3	2	
29	T. J. L.	50	Many years	Butcher	August 24-30 . . .	October 1	3	2	1
30	C. W. W.	26	22	Farmer	August 15-20 . .	October 1	2	1	
31	W. R.	60	42	Paper Maker . .	August 20 . . .	Hard frost	3	1	
32	J. S.	38	31	Bank Officer . .	August 15-24 . .	October 1	3	3	
33	T.	26	21	Clergyman . . .	August 24-31 . .	Frosty nights	3	2	
34	L. E.	27	19	Merchant . . .	August 18	Frosty nights	3	3	
35	C. H.	65	Early Youth	. . . . .	August 21	October 1	3	2	
36	H. G. F.	24	8	Merchant . . .	August 19-21 . .	First hard frost	3	0	
37	F. B. F.	45	20		August 20	October 1	3	2	
38	G. T.	46	13	Brick Maker . .	August 20-24 . . .	October 1	3	3	
39	W. A. P.	21	5	Student	August 10	Last week in September	3	2	
40	E. C. F.	34	Infancy	Merchant . . .	August 20-27 . . .	September 10-20	3	0	
41	J. W. D.	40	19	Merchant . . .	August 20 . . .	October 1	3	2	
42	E. P.	49	22	Physician . . .	August 20	First frost	3	2	
43	G. H. H.	35	24	Teacher	August 28	First frost	3	3	
44	J. T. H.	–	–	Engineer . . .	August 27	In six or eight weeks	–	–	
45	C. W.	25	14	Student	About August 15	Six weeks	3	2	
46	F. H.	–	23	Manufacturer . .	August 11-15 . . .	First week in October	2	1	
47	J. A. W.	33	4	Bookbinder . . .	August 20	October 1	3	3	
48	B. S. H.	44	14	Clergyman . . .	August 20	Six weeks	3	0	
49	J. B. F. T.	34	7 or 8	Merchant . . .	August 15	Two months	3	2	
50	J. W.	57	52	Prof. of Anatomy	Last week in Aug.	October 1	3	2	
51	E. F.	49	25	Clergyman . . .	August 15	First frost	3	3	
52	T. H. M.	46	41	Manufacturer . .	August 21	September 25	2	1	
53	J. N. W.	58	35	Lawyer	August 22	September 21	3	3	
54	M. H.	52	45	Banker	August 20, 21 . .	Four weeks	3	2	
55	A. C. D.	42	7	Merchant . . .	August 20	September 25	3	1	

OBSERVATIONS.	INFLUENCE OF RESIDENCE OR LOCALITY.
sthmatic, and died of phthisis	Entirely relieved in Switzerland, London, England, and White Mountains; very little relief at sea-side.
and a brother's son have Autumnal Catarrh	Two years in Europe, no catarrh: 1863, in the Tyrol, had symptoms one hour only.
prolonged bronchitis. A brother has Autumnal Catarrh . .	Entire relief at Gorham, Jefferson Hill, Glen House; somewhat relieved at Profile House, and Mt. Mansfield in Green Mountains; no relief at North Conway.
l aunt has catarrh in autumn	Entire relief in England and Highlands of Scotland: at sea; at Glen House, Profile House; at Crawford's; aggravated at Cape May.
. . . .	No relief at sea-side nor Conway, N. H.; relieved at Gorham; entire relief at Success.
ack very severe. Gradually disappeared after several years . .	
apoplexy at the age of sixty-nine	Entire relief in Scotland in 1839; in White Mountains from August 17, 1851, till August 26, and in Franklin, till September 8. Attacked next day immediately on arrival in Boston.
disease of brain and cirrhosis of liver	
forty-four of cardiac disease	Entire relief for nine years in St. Paul, Minn ; during this period was one year, in September, in Cambridge, Mass., and had catarrh.
two brothers, one sister, one son, have Autumnal Catarrh: one ter has June Catarrh.	Entire relief at Gorham and Glen House, and England. No relief at Profile House, Crawford's, Mt. Monadnock, N. H., nor sea-coast.
ld: eyes irritated in hay-field and by hay in the barn; cannot it in September except where he is free from catarrh.	Some relief at Cape Cod: usually entire relief at White Mountains; relief after crossing the Mississippi on the way to San Francisco.
r in New York suffers severely from Autumnal Catarrh . . .	In White Mountains eight years, with entire relief; in 1860 was in England, in autumn, with entire relief.
has Autumnal Catarrh. (No. 24.)	Suffers most at sea-coast: complete relief at Jefferson Hill, Glen House, and Gorham; slight relief at North Conway.
very severe from the first	Suffered severely at Mt. Monadnock and Crawford House: complete relief three last years at Glen House, Gorham, and England.
t severe generally	1867, August 17, catarrh ceased at Littleton on way to Dublin, N. H., and returned at same place on the way home, where it was severe.
ase: keeps bed; has night sweats and is much reduced in flesh rength.	Entire relief at Gorham; worse at Isles of Shoals.
attend to his occupation through attack	
has had Autumnal Catarrh eight to ten years, now eighty-one ld: sister has June Catarrh.	Complete relief during the two weeks he was in Gorham, in 1866.
er 1865, had pneumonia	No relief at sea-shore.
r children: one daughter has Antumnal Catarrh, which comes within a few hours of her father's attack.	
tarrh severe	Complete relief at Catskill Mountain and western New York.
. . . .	While residing in New Ipswich, N. H., relieved by going to Boston: resided at Saco, Me., on sea-coast, fifteen years: attacks regular but less severe.
vere case; kept bed in a dark room in former years, of late less . Cousin has Autumnal Catarrh. (No. 13.)	Complete relief at Gorham, Glen House, Crawford's, and Peterboro', Madison Co., N. Y.: no relief at Sharon Springs, or Isles of Shoals.
tarrh of late years continues longer in a modified degree . .	Relief in Highlands of Georgia, and north side of White Mountains; no relief at Franconia.
	Eight successive years at White Mountains, Gorham, Glen House, and vicinity: always relief—generally complete.
d action of heart during attack	Relief at Glen House: Island of Mackinaw.
believed to commence the same day and same hour each year.	Suffered most severely while transportation agent on a railway.
March, 1851, with cardiac symptoms and effusion into pleura, dium, and brain. Mother, son, and granddaughter have Autum ttarrh.	Returning from Europe, landed in Boston October 1, well; in two days had catarrh.
	No catarrh while for several successive years he was in Muscatine, Iowa; returning to Somerville, Mass., disease reappeared in less severe form.
ur attack began September 5. Niece has Autumnal Catarrh reat Gorham and Quebec.	1867, at Gorham: all symptoms relieved.
severe case	Entire relief at Quebec and Gorham.
	1867, August 17, arrived at Gorham: complete relief same day.
ne Cold from early youth until four years ago. Was one year in ne in June. No catarrh.	1867, September 4, at Gorham, relief immediate, and in two or three days complete: no relief at Fire Island or Catskill Mountains.
of eyes begins August 1	1867, complete relief at Summit House and Glen.
	Escaped catarrh in England; relieved at Long Branch.
with first hard frost. Resides on Hudson River ten miles from ill House.	Relief at Eastport and Houlton, Me.
re to hay in barn produces sneezing	In 1858, was in England, Ireland, and Scotland, in August and September complete relief; no relief in Maryland and Virginia in 1863, 1864.
	Complete relief at Gorham, in 1868; no relief at Catskill Mountain House nor at sea-side.
vere case	Complete relief in England, near Manchester, in 1858, and in Scotland, near Balmoral, in 1859; relief in Halifax, N. S., and at White Mountains, in 1868.
three years had catarrh while roses were in bloom; none since rance of Autumnal Catarrh	Has always resided in Boston and vicinity.
severe case with much asthma	Complete relief at White Mountains and Canada; no relief at sea-side.
cceases in St. Louis later than in Neretta; frost later in St. than Neretta.	1867-1870, relief at northwest side of White Mts.; no relief at sea-side.
	In 1862 escaped catarrh in Salem, Mass.; this the only year; no relief at St. Louis.
relieved while suffering from diarrhœa	Complete relief in Nova Scotia and three years while in Montana, U. S., and Colorado: no relief at Frostburg, Md., 1,050 feet above tide.
ncle had Autumnal Catarrh forty years, beginning at thirty . .	Relieved two years at Port Royal and at White Mountains; less severe at sea-side.
	Relief at White Mountains: no relief at sea-side.
. . . .	Relieved at Lakes Umbagog, Memphramagog in Maine, and at Littleton and Whitefield.
. . . .	Relieved at Catskill Mountains and in Scotland in 1866.
. . . .	Complete relief at Adirondac Mountains: some relief at sea-side; no relief at Profile House in 1858.
. . . .	Relief at Glen: none at Mt. Desert, but relieved while on an island two miles distant.
arents had catarrh; mother more severely, but neither periodically	Relieved at Gorham, while in Northern Germany and in central England.
	Escaped catarrh in England and in Europe one year; relieved at Gorham, 1871.
ents his case as very severe in all its symptoms	Was well in Switzerland and Italy in 1870; some relief at Fire Island, much greater relief at Glen House in 1871.
. . . .	Well in France and Switzerland, 1867-1869; well at Glen House.
. . . .	Was relieved at Bethlehem, near White Mountains.

No.	Name.	Age when First Attacked.	Number of Annual Attacks.	ANNUAL ATTACK.		Head Symptoms.	Chest Symptoms.		
				Beginning.	End.		Cough.	Asthma.	
56	Mrs. H.	44	25	August 24	October 1	2	3	2	Chronic bronchitis for ten ... continuing into the wint... Cold in early life, afterw...
57	Mrs. A. H.	28	24	Third week in Aug.	First frost	3	2	2	Chronic affection of nasal ... mencement of Autumna...
58	Mrs. J. B.	32	14	August 17	October 1	3	2	0	June cold from sixteen to ... Catarrh; a sister has Ju... land or on the Continent
59	Mrs. S. B.	-	-	August 20	October 1	3	3	0	Had June cold before Aut...
60	Mrs. G. D.	20	8	August 15-18	October 1	3	3	3	
61	Mrs. S. B. B.	43	25	August 23	October 1	2	1	3	Gradual diminution in sev...
62	Mrs. J. H. D.	21	9	August 15-20	First week in October	2	3	3	Had catarrh in June three... England, and has not re...
63	Miss A.	26	12	August 15-24	October 1	3	1	3	Had pneumonia in Septen
64	Mrs. B.	46	4	About August 23	First frost	3	2	0	
65	Mrs. M. J. M.	16	22	August 17-24	October 1	3	3	0	June Catarrh till five year...
66	C. C.	27	8	August 15-20	First frost	3	3	3	Autumnal Catarrh; arrest... ing three days; on recov
67	Mrs. D.	33	10	August 20	October 1	3	2	0	...
68	Mrs. C.	-	20	August 17	First frost	1	-	-	...
69	Miss E. W.	39	7	August 25-31		1	2	0	Case generally mild ...
	Miss H. W.	25	11	August 20	October 1	3	3	0	
	Mrs. W. B.	27	25	August 20	October 10	3	3	3	Mother died at seventy-ni... verity gradually.
	Miss A.	24	11	August 19	September 27	3	1	3	...
	Mrs. F. A. B.	22	24	Fourth week in Aug.	First frost	3	2	2	...
	Miss. A. C. D.	24	8	August 20	Fourth week in September	3	0	0	...
75	Mrs. S. B.	12	33	August 20	First frost	3	3	3	...
76 77	Mrs. S. D. P.	13	25	August 23	First frost	3	3	3	Mother had Autumnal Ca...
	Mrs. R.	30	23	August 20	Last days of Sept., first days of Oct.	3	3	3	...
	Miss S. W.	-	5	August 16-20	November 1	3	3	-	Cannot eat peaches or tom...
	Miss B.	32	5	August 19, 20	September 25	3	1	0	
	Mrs. F.	21	6	August 11, 12	October 1	3	2	0	The affection of the eyes ...
	Mrs. G.	40	10	August 17, 18	September 25	1	3	1	Father, two brothers, and ... critical period.

of severity. 1, *mild;* 2, *moderate;* 3, *severe :* 0, *wanting.*

_LES.

OBSERVATIONS.	INFLUENCE OF RESIDENCE OR LOCALITY.
teen years, gradually increasing in severity, the cough lied suddenly December 31, 1866. Daughter had Rose Autumnal Catarrh.	Relieved entirely at White Mountains; relieved in Boston.
ous membrane; June Cold ten years; ceased with com-tarrh.	Complete relief at Gorham, and in 1869 at Carrol, N. H.; some relief at sea-side.
y-two; nearly ceased at commencement of Autumnal)ld. No June Cold during four years while in Eng-	Complete relief at White Mountains and Bethel, and during three years at sea-side.
	Relieved at Gorham: attacks less severe since.
al Catarrh; attacks produced by flowers and peaches .	Complete relief at White Mountain Notch; partial relief at Profile House; in 1868 no relief at Jefferson Hill; no relief at sea-side.
· of symptoms	Less severe in Boston than in the country.
s in succession; ceased during two years' residence in ared since return home.	Complete relief at Glen House; partial relief at Profile House: complete relief during passage from Liverpool to New York; no relief at Catskill Mountains.
1862	Complete relief at Gorham, in 1866; health improved during following year.
)	Complete relief at Gorham, in 1866 and 1847; some relief at sea-coast.
, since then Autumnal Catarrh	1866 and 1867 at Gorham with complete relief.
a September during an attack of cholera morbus, last-evere attack of asthma.	
. . . .	Much relieved in Lake Superior region.
. . . .	Entirely relieved in Dublin, N. H., Gorham, and Glen. . . . .
nad Autumnal Catarrh most of life; diminished in se-	Worse in the country than in Cambridge: complete relief in Gorham.
. . . .	Complete relief for eleven years at Profile House, Crawford's, and Glen House.
. . . .	Relief at Gorham; no relief at sea-coast.
. . . .	Relieved in the Glen; no relief at sea-coast; relieved in New York.
. . . .	Landed in New York from Liverpool, September 16; catarrh commenced same day; catarrh at St. Louis, Missouri, five years in succession.
. . . .	Relief at Glen House, 1864 and 1865; no relief at Crawford's or Profile, nor at Crescent, in the Alleghanies of Virginia.
till sixty-four years of age	Complete relief at Waumbec House two years: one year escaped at Beverly Farms, Ms.
. . . .	No catarrh at sea or in Manilla; some catarrh sensations in Macao; decided relief at Gorham.
s at home; can eat them freely at the White Mountains	Relieved at Glen House, at Gorham, and the Waumbec; has visited mountains past three years.
severe	Much relieved at Glen House, and at Murray Bay, on the St. Lawrence, below Quebec.
. . . .	Somewhat relieved at Long Branch; three years in Europe quite well; quite well at the Glen House.
ister died of consumption; one brother has asthma at	Well at Glen House.

HEIGHTS OF VILLAGES AND HOTELS IN NON-CATARRHAL RE-GIONS AND THEIR VICINITY.

Taken principally from "Appalachian Mountain System," by Professor Arnold Guyot, New Haven, 1861, and "Gazetteer of New York," by J. H. French.

Those marked with * are considered safe places of resort; those marked †
are doubtful.

The heights are given in English feet, above mean tide water.
They are all reduced to the ground, or, for the rivers, to the level of
the water.

CULMINATING REGION OF THE NORTHERN SECTION.

WHITE MOUNTAINS AND VICINITY.

Western Slope. — Valley of the Ammonoosuc.

Connecticut River junction with Wells River	407
Bath Village	521
Lisbon Village	577
Littleton, Railroad Station	817
*Whitefield, summit between Littleton and Lancaster	1,057
*Whitefield Village	957
*Waumbec House	1,248
Lancaster Village	860
Israel River, Lancaster Bridge, St. Lawrence and Atlantic Railroad	849
*Bethlehem Village	1,450
*Carrol House	1,428
*Bethlehem Bridge on the Ammonoosuc	1,221
*Brabrook's Hotel	1,551
*Fabyan's Hotel (old house now burnt)	1,583
*Crawford Hotel (Crawford House); White Mountain Notch	1,920
*White Mountain House	1,568
*Franconia Village, Iron Foundry	921
*Gilmanton Hill, summit between Franconia and Littleton	1,329

11

*Franconia Valley, crossing of road to Bethlehem	979
*Franconia Notch, Profile House	1,974
*Franconia Notch, height of land towards Franconia	2,014
*Echo Lake	1,926
*Cherry Mountain, Summit Road	2,192
*Cabin, foot of Lafayette Mountain	1,780
*Flume House, road front of the Hotel	1,431
Thornton, road opposite the Post-office	1,223·
Plymouth Railroad Station	473

Eastern Slope — Valley of the Saco.

*Notch of White Mountains, Crawford House	1,920
*The Notch	1,904
*Willey House, road opposite the hotel	1,335
*Old Crawford's, or Davis's Hotel	986
Hart's location, Farm junction Sawyer's River	880
Upper Bartlett Post-office	644
South Conway Post-office	450

Valleys of Ellis and Sawyer's River.

Jackson Village, hotel foot of the Falls	771
*Pinkham Notch, summit near Glen Ellis Falls	2,018
*Junction of Carrigain Brook and Sawyer's River	1,494

Northern Slope.

*Mount Washington, spirit level, 6,285, 6,293; barometer, 6,291; average	6,289
*Gorham, N. H., Railroad Station, St. Lawrence & Atlantic Railroad	802
*Randolph Hill	1,400
*Glenhouse Hotel	1,632
*Bowman's Place, Summit Road, between Moose and Israel Rivers	1,446
*Lowest Summit, Railroad Summit, between Moose and Israel Rivers	1,473

GROUP OF FRANCONIA MOUNTAINS.

Highest farm foot of Moose Hillock, south	1,681
Concord, N. H., Railroad Station	237
Lake Winnipiseogee; mean level of the interior valleys of N. H.	501
Conway Intervale, Saco Valley	471

Senter House at Centre Harbor, Lake Winni-
piseogce 553
*North Wakefield, Railroad summit . . 700

GREEN MOUNTAINS.

†Manchester Railroad Station 713
†Manchester Village Court-house . . . 864
Rutland Railroad Station 530
Waterbury Railroad Station . . . 425
*Mansfield Mountain House 4,000
*Stow Village, foot of Mount Mansfield . . 700
Williamstown, Vt. 1,590
Craftsbury, Vt. 1,158
Berkshire Hills, Mass. 1,500
Pass of Berkshire Hills. (Lowest Pass to Hud-
son River) 1,440
Stockbridge, Mass. 1,400
†Mount Tom, Connecticut River . . . 1,214
Williamstown College 930
Eastern hills of Massachusetts. Average of
highest range east of Connecticut . . 1,000
Worcester. Average of Eastern Massachusetts 536

EAST OF WHITE MOUNTAINS.

*Houlton, general level, inland 620
*Fort Fairfield, Valley of St. John River . 415
*Port Kent, Valley of Aroostook River . . 575
*Moosehead Lake, Interior Valley . . 1,000

PLATEAU AND MOUNTAINS OF ADIRONDAC.

Lake Champlain, mean level 93
Crown Point Tavern 206
Bradford farm, road summit 695
*Amyhill summit road 614
*Buckhollow Hamlet, water of Putnam Creek . 719
*Penfield, water of Putnam Creek . . 910
*Hammond's Furnace 1,132
*Paradox Creek, Hammond's saw-mill . . 911
*Sturtevant's Mill, Mud Creek 1,113
*French's farm, road before 1,962
*Grand Boreas River, bridge 1,736
*Adirondac Village, or McIntyre's Iron Works
hotel 1,785
*Lake Colden· 2,786

NEW YORK AND OHIO PLATEAU.

Mean altitude of the Plateau	2,000
Mean altitude of Valleys	1,500
*Catskill Mountain	3,432
*Catskill Mountain House, above Hudson River	3,212
*Cazenovia, Madison County	1,260
*Peterboro', Smithfield, Madison County	1,200
*Madison County	1,400–2,000
*Madison County Valley	900–1,200
*Courtland County, northern part a high plateau	1,100–1,200
*Courtland County Hills	1,600–2,100
*Horner	1,500
*Preble	1,700
*Solon	1,400
*Virgil	1,600
*Chemung County	1,300–1,500
*Steuben County	2,500
*Corning	928
*Bath	1,090
*Arkport	963
*Alleghany County	2,000–2,500
*Alleghany County Valleys	1,500–1,700
*Angelica	1,430
*Wellsville	1,480
*Little Genesee	1,500
*Cattaraugus County, summits	2,500–3,000
*Cattaraugus County, valleys	1,200–1,700
*Olean	1,280
*Franklin	1,580
*Ellicottville	1,283
*Chatauque County	1,300
*Charlotte, Carroll, Busti, Arkwright	1,500
*Ellery, Gerry, and Harmony	1,400
*Island of Mackinaw, between Lake Huron and Lake Michigan	728

ALLEGHANY MOUNTAINS.

*Frostburg, Maryland	1,792
*West Point	1,160
*Meadville, Pennsylvania	1,088

GREAT LAKES.

Lake Superior	641
Lake Huron	596
Lake Michigan	600
Lake Erie	565
Lake Ontario	231

MISSISSIPPI RIVER.

St. Louis, Missouri	481
*Muscatine, Iowa	585
*St. Paul, Minnesota	820

In the maps the uncolored space represents regions which are believed to be free from Autumnal Catarrh.

INDEX.

———

Adirondac Mountains, safe place of resort, 71.

Age as a cause of catarrh, 79.

Air, draught of, produces attacks of sneeezing, 12.

Alæ of nose, inflammation of, 24.

Alpine House, White Mountain region, a safe place of resort, 68.

Ambrosia artemisiæfolia, time of flowering of, 35; an active cause of paroxysms, 100; not a cause of the disease, 101; experiments with, 101 note, 102; Dr. Gray on geographical distribution of, 102 note.

Animals as a cause of catarrh, 105; of asthma, 107.

Appetite diminished, 27.

Apple, time of flowering, 37 note.

Ascaris megalocephala, effects of, 106 note.

Asthma produced by animal emanations, 107.

Asthma, when occurring, 20; not a constant symptom, 21; asthmatic stage, 45.

Asthma, treatment of, 132.

Atkins, E. F., 14 note; his journey from Boston to San Francisco during the period of Autumnal Catarrh, 57 note.

Autumnal Catarrh, when first described, 2; why so named, 4; countries in which it does not exist, 50; disease of temperate climates, 59; not cured by drugs, 79; persists through life, 78.

Bacteria as a cause of "Hay Fever," Helmholtz on, 105 note.

Bacteria, existence in air and human body, 109; supposed to be a cause of disease, 109 note.

Bacteria, Professor Wyman's experiments on, 110 note.

Bancroft, Mrs., 31 note.

Bachelder, Samuel, relieved partially at sea-shore, 62 note, 11 note, 38 note, 34 note.

Bastian, H. Charlton, effects of *Ascaris megalocephala* on, 106 note.

Bears eat tobacco, 87 note.

Beal, Lionel S., on diseased germs, 109.

Beecher, Rev. H. W., description of symptoms in his own case, 10 note, 17 note, 18 note, 20 note, 24 note, 25 note, 29 note, 30 note, 44.

Beecher, Rev. Henry Ward, illustrative case, 141.

Beer Plant of California, when dried retains its vitality, 110.

Beginning of Autumnal Catarrh, date of, 36.

Berkshire Hills, in Mass., not safe, 73.

Bernard, Claude, lectures on the nervous system, 87 note.

Bethel, Maine, on the border of non-catarrhal region, 71.